Praise for THE PROMISE OF POTENTIAL

"Jodi Davis has it just right: begin with the deepest dynamics of self, then move ahead into action and leadership. She does not just tell us *what* to change. Jodi helps us begin our own journey with powerful exercises, questions and resources. Take this book seriously and potential will be more than a promise; it will start to become a reality."

Don M. Frick, Ph.D.
Author of *Robert K. Greenleaf: A Life of Servant Leadership*

"This book is the definitive guide to creating more of what you want in your life and work! Jodi has captured the essence of potential and how to create a path for seeing it, reaching it, and celebrating it."

Mark LeBlanc
Author of *Growing Your Business!*
2007-2008 President, National Speakers Association

"*The Promise of Potential* is a must-read for anyone who has ever wondered about life and all its potential. Answering the questions moves you toward action, and once your true self is revealed to you, nothing can stop you from living the life you imagine."

Tené Wells
President, WomenVenture

"This book is for any reader – male or female, young or old, successful or struggling – who is open to sound guidance for enhancing self-awareness, exploring emotional needs, expanding vision, and taking action to achieve his or her full potential."

Carolyn Riley
2007 Chairperson of the Board of Directors,
Children's Cancer Research Fund

"Jodi Davis is like that wise and caring aunt who is happy to share personal wisdom with those young-at-heart willing to hear it. She shares the fruit of discovery from her own journey and lets us feel safe and accepted, while she takes us through a similar growth spurt. In *The Promise of Potential* she lays out a clear, concise method and remarkable workbook so we can proceed to live our lives with authenticity and genuine productivity.... A gold medal for Jodi Davis!"

John Naber
Olympic Gold Medal Swimming Champion,
Author of *Awaken the Olympian Within*

"*The Promise of Potential* is a book I would recommend to young professionals for its wisdom and its practicality. Jodi Davis has crafted a work that provides concise and encouraging methods for achieving personal and professional success, and it feels like a good friend is cheering you on."

André Lewis
Senior Vice President, RBC Dain Rauscher

"Jodi Davis offers well-framed insights for anyone who has made a commitment to explore the fullness of who they are. With an approach that's both sensitive and sensible, this pragmatic work becomes an interpreter, a personal coach, and a champion for its readers."

Betsy Buckley
CEO of What Matters,
Author of *The Power of Why* and *Sell More, Sell Inside First,*
and creator of the EveryDayRain™ Success System

"*The Promise of Potential* reminds us to be our true self. Jodi Davis is right on target! She encourages us to live our life with the vision of how we want to be remembered."

Jackie Pflug
Speaker, Airline Hijacking Survivor,
and author of *Miles to Go Before I Sleep*

THE PROMISE
OF POTENTIAL

When you want more for your life

JODI DAVIS

JD Coaching and Consulting, Minneapolis, MN 55401

Printed in the United States of America

ISBN 978-1-60461-877-8

Book design and typesetting: Gretchen Westbrock, Adsoka
Cover design: Thom Sandberg
Cover photography: Mark LaFavor

First Printing: November 2007

JD Coaching and Consulting
49 North Fourth Avenue, Suite #103
Minneapolis, MN 55401
www.JodiDavis.com

For information, updates or to order additional copies visit www.ThePromiseOfPotential.com

Dedicated to my children and grandchildren
who inspire me to achieve
the promise of my potential.

TABLE OF CONTENTS

ACKNOWLEDGMENTS

To Mark LeBlanc, my extraordinary entrepreneur coach and dear friend, who inspired and encouraged me to look deep within myself for the insights and knowledge to create a book that will allow me and others to reach our fullest potential.

To Jason Inskeep and the awesome Adsoka team for their generous contribution of time, professionalism, and savvy marketing communications expertise – thank you for your commitment to developing my book's potential.

To Thom Sandberg for your radiant cover. You artfully captured the essence of my book with your beautiful design. What a gem!

To Todd Berntson whose guidance took my writing to a higher level.

To Carolyn Riley, the regal quintessential Comma Queen, whose meticulous command of language and writing proofed and polished every page!

To John Naber for permission to use your inspiring story – I am grateful for your gifted insights after reading early drafts of my manuscript. You improved the book's quality and gave it the potential for a *literary* Gold Medal.

To Will Stockton and Marjorie Herdes for embracing my desire to use the Mobius Model in my work. Thank you for your understanding as I develop my possibilities! To Jeff Pauley who heightened my appreciation for exemplary leadership.

To my clients and close friends whose real-life stories contributed to the creation of practical applications that support the premises of this book.

A special thank you to: André Lewis, Kathleen McCartin, Betsy Buckley, Mike Goldstein, Don Frick, Dan McCormick, Tené Wells, and Jackie Pflug. Thank you so much for your enthusiasm in reading my manuscript, for your sensitive comments, and for your friendship, without which I would not be as proud of this accomplishment nor as hopeful for the book's promise of success.

Thank you!

Foreword

Each of us is a unique being – a magnificent expression of the Universe. When born, we are granted the opportunity of a lifetime – an opportunity to realize our true self and our potential. At the moment of our birth, we embark on a lifelong journey of discovery. The path we take is filled with many choices, great possibility and immense power.

The journey may be exhilarating and motivate us to explore many diverse passages. Alternatively, our road may be lonely, and it may not be easy to follow. The journey does not come with directions. The course through life may be steep, winding, or it may even lead us into darkness and despair. But with each step forward, we must keep in mind that we are not really alone. As we journey, in the best outcomes, we find our contentment and peace.

If we follow the road with an open heart, it will take us to a place where we can find truth. The true essence of our life comes from first looking deep within our being to discover ourselves. We must search to see the gems that make us unique. As human beings, creations of the Universe, we are treasures of the Earth. Each of us comes with unique talents, strengths, needs and complex characteristics. We are multifaceted, extraordinary individuals, each possessing life's inherent gift of great potential.

We are like diamonds, the most precious of gems. Diamonds are valued for their strength, brilliance, uniqueness and beauty. Just like mining for diamonds, we need to dig deep to know ourselves. If we invest in discovering our truth and developing our visions – for all we want to be – we, too, can realize our strength and brilliance. We, too, can radiate and shine.

To know who we are, to accept who we are, and to live authentically is to treasure our inner diamond and ourselves. There are many magnificent roads that can lead to a life of fulfillment. And there are several ways we can prepare for our passage and ensure its success. Our life is merely a journey and an exploration of our potential. Each step we take is an opportunity for growth and development. The passageway begins with awareness.

In my lifetime, I have traversed many different roads – some long, some lonely, some very difficult, and some extraordinarily rewarding. I learned that like the diamonds I adore, I am multifaceted and complex. I have come to know my gifts, and yet at times I have felt like a rough diamond in need of polishing. While I often felt beautifully radiant, I sometimes knew I needed more clarity to shine.

The good times were easy – dreams were delivered as glorious accomplishments. But it was during my most difficult moments that I had to be a "rock solid diamond" and tenaciously draw on my inner strength to pull me through. During these times, with deep soul searching and personal reflection, I learned valuable lessons.

My most profound insight was accepting my own imperfections and recognizing that all diamonds, regardless of their flaws, are treasured gems. This realization took immense courage – courage that was packaged in pain and sometimes in sadness. When the tears dried, I saw with greater clarity the value of what I had learned. I have come to appreciate that to be successful – in our work, in our relationships, and in our lives – we need courage and confidence to pursue our path to power.

The two-year process of writing this book was a journey in itself. I had already learned so much from my education, professional career, and training as an executive coach. But it took deep meditative reflection during these past two years to uncover the secrets for living a life of fulfillment and inner peace.

The process centered on *awareness* of self. I knew that my dreams would remain unfulfilled and happiness would elude me if I did not embrace my identity – with all of its multifaceted gems and imperfections. I came to understand it was imperative that I know my truth. I needed to trust my truth, for only then would I be able to unleash my potential and live an empowered life.

As any road warrior knows, one must have a destination in mind to chart his or her course. To better serve me on my path to power, I sharpened my ability to create and manifest the vision for my life. I drew upon the gifts that I had been given and the teachings embedded in my life experiences to craft an action plan for achieving my dreams. The excursion was designed to take me from authenticity to action. I propelled myself toward my vision.

The Promise of Potential was part of my transcendence. This book was written first for me – and then for you. The experience has been transformational, and I want to share the lessons I have learned. My journey brought with it valuable teachings from a number of recognized experts, each of whom made incredible contributions to the study of individual development. As Isaac Newton said, "If I have seen further, it is by standing on the shoulders of giants." My book contains newly synthesized material of substance that will hopefully help you appreciate your potential.

To acknowledge some of the experts who contributed to my development and growth, I have referenced additional resources throughout the book in a special section labeled **Links to Potential**. If you would like more information on a particular topic, you may find some of these listings (Websites, books, organizations, etc.) helpful as you develop your own potential.

Success in this journey results from a confluence of important characteristics: **understanding**, **wisdom**, **strength** and **faith**. I have come to understand what it takes to have courage and confidence on the path to realizing one's potential.

Hopefully, the wisdom I have gained from my own journey will give you strength as you go through yours. With the stories, lessons and tools offered in this book, you will feel like you have your own personal coach in your back pocket!

If you carefully and persistently read each chapter and complete the exercises in this book, you will hopefully create a comprehensive understanding of who you are and what you desire most for your life. If you are like many people, you may dislike completing workbook exercises. While I appreciate how you might feel and have even shared these sentiments in the past, I encourage you to make the effort to perform the recommended activities in this book.

Often, the people who are most successful in incorporating new behaviors into their lives do so because of the actions they take to learn and practice different techniques. Action creates change, and the exercises in this book are actions that can bring about change in your life. For example, the techniques presented in the Communication and Action Exercises chapters should provide you with an outline to facilitate putting your desire into action. I trust that the ideas presented will enhance your confidence and give you more courage to be yourself.

These are the gifts that I want to pass on to you, my reader, to help you gain awareness of your talents, values and goals as you pursue your path to power. I offer you the treasures I have found in polishing my own diamond so that you may discover yours. With your own dreams in mind, with your life challenges and special purpose, I invite you to look inside your heart, reach into your soul, and have faith that you have everything you need to achieve the promise of your potential.

– Jodi Davis

BECOMING SENTIENT

I discovered the word "sentient" one day when I was searching the thesaurus on my computer for a word that could connect two seemingly opposing concepts: intellect and intuition. The adjective *sentient* means "capable of sensation or feeling, conscious or aware of something." The thesaurus relates it to words like conscious, aware, attentive, alert, observant, perceptive and sensitive. Derived from the 17th century Latin word *sentiens* and *sentire*, meaning "to feel," the word sentient "felt" like it had special meaning for me. To me, sentient simply means "awareness."

Awareness is the first step to self-acceptance, which is a key to unlocking potential. A sentient being ultimately transcends his or her individual needs to give back and help others. The full expression of being sentient means we are one with our truth. We must own our truth and trust our truth. We have to live our truth – every day.

There are four basic essentials of being sentient. They include knowledge and awareness of our: Identity, Authenticity, Vision and Action. **Identity (I am)** is the term for how you see yourself. It is comprised of two parts: your *internal* identity – innate talents, gifts and characteristics, and your *external* identity – the roles or labels that society bestows upon you.

All people have these external components of identity, which are comprised of many cultural descriptors relating to their nationality, race, religion, gender and family position. It is easy to understand why so many of us relate our identity to our cultural group, family role or job title. However, many people stop with these external definitions for who they are, and in doing so, disregard the other *(internal)* part of their identity. When identity is drawn from the external definitions only, people will tend to seek something else to make them feel whole – connections, relationships and accomplishments.

All of us also have natural gifts, talents, strengths and capabilities that make up our internal identity. This is the aspect of identity that needs to be fostered.

Awareness of your internal identity involves looking inside yourself and appreciating the unique characteristics that define the true you. *What are the values and beliefs ingrained in how you operate? What are the special gifts that you bring to this lifetime to share? What are the challenges you face, the lessons you need to learn, the circumstances that will allow you to live a life of purpose that manifests your highest ideals?*

Embracing your full identity comes from the melding of both internal and external elements. When identity is formed from both components, individuals are more apt to appreciate their uniqueness and the full sense of what makes them whole. The formation of identity is an evolutionary process that balances the internal and external sources of that which defines who we are. Embracing both parts of our identity allows us to associate with others *and* to be uniquely individual. As human beings, we are the totality of our cultural and societal classifications *together with* our distinctive physical, emotional, intellectual and spiritual characteristics.

> **Embracing your full identity comes from the melding of both internal and external elements.**

Identity, in the full awareness model, is the foundation for who you "are" – not what you "do" or what you "have." With a complete sense of identity, you are never second best because you are a unique being. When you accept yourself as unique, you are less likely to fall into the comparison trap, and when you embrace your whole identity, your motivation to achieve emanates from within. With this awareness of your identity, striving to reach your potential comes from an internal motivation, and you are free to just *be*.

Awareness of your identity spawns your creativity, your passion, your energy and attraction, and your vision. That is YOU. It is empowering to tap into your internal gifts and talents. This self-knowledge helps you be on your power base. This is the central stance from which you draw your strength and stability. When you are on your power base, there is a solid foundation, and you are less likely to falter. To be fully sentient is to be empowered by living life from your power base. From this posture, you are in a better position to resist outside forces that threaten to move you off-center as you pursue fulfillment of your potential.

Authenticity (I need) is the outward projection of your identity. Authenticity is the expression of your truth. It is what you project. It is how you live your life in accordance with your values and your truth. Those who are authentic don't change themselves to gain someone's approval; they are who they are, and they accept the natural rewards and consequences.

Whatever you project is what you will attract. When you are authentic, you will tend to attract people who and circumstances that support you. If you are not authentic, or not real, you will tend to attract that which supports your false identity. In essence, you will sabotage the positive attraction forces that support your ability to achieve your potential.

Why would someone choose not to be authentic? Individuals often choose to try to be someone they are not so that they will be accepted by others. When we do this, we dismiss our true identity and take on the characteristics of others. In this position, we are second best. We are trying to be like someone else, and we lose our identity in the process of trying to be accepted. When we consciously believe someone else has something we want, or is someone we want to be, we give away our power. Living authentically is an important aspect of developing yourself and fulfilling your potential.

Vision (I want) is the collective expression of what you want – your dreams, goals and aspirations. It describes what you want to have and what you want to become. Creating your vision is critical for your ability to reach your potential. With a clear vision of what you desire, it becomes easier to pull away from that which is undesirable or unfulfilling in your life. The magnetism of your vision allows you to spend your energy in positive desire instead of in the pain of a negative circumstance.

Creating a vision can be analogous to planning a vacation. When you decide to go on a trip, you usually have an exciting destination in mind. The anticipation of knowing where you are going fuels your energy and enthusiasm to organize and pack for the vacation. In the same way, a visualization of where you want to be helps you prepare for the journey and enhances your potential for fulfillment.

Actions (I will) are the process of making your vision a reality. To take action, or to act, means to proceed, move toward, take steps, or to do something. It also means to accomplish and achieve. Your actions are the steps that move you toward your vision. Your actions bring together the elements of who you are and what you want. The successful attainment of your potential begins with living life authentically, consistent with your values and identity. Your actions need to be aligned with your authentic self; your actions will determine whether or not you fulfill your higher purpose and add depth to your life experience.

A final note on being sentient: *Integration.* The investment in developing our awareness of our identity, authenticity, vision and action does not happen in a vacuum or sterile bubble. We are multifaceted beings who live in a complex world. As individuals we must integrate our head, our heart and our spirit (intuition) to reach our full potential.

We often need support to stay aligned with our truth. This is where our sources of personal power – loved ones, advocates, special friends and mentors can offer us the guidance necessary to stay focused on our truth. These supporters are universal gifts that are offered to each of us. Awareness of your *Partners in Power*, and knowing how to tap into their strength, is vital to achieving your potential.

Life journeys frequently encompass explorations that are both exciting and uncomfortable. That which is uncomfortable may be the most exciting! The challenges you face may spawn your greatest growth. The lessons imbedded in the difficult moments may be the most valuable lessons of all.

Awareness of self, and becoming sentient, is a lifelong process; there is no beginning and no end. We discover more about ourselves each and every day. The beauty is in the process itself – the drilling down to reach our core. As we develop and grow to achieve our vision, we are like delicate budding flowers searching for the nourishing energy that makes us blossom and radiate life's most powerful force – our potential.

I AM

Identity

Our individual DNA and our unique fingerprints serve to identify us as individuals unique among all other beings. We go through life with personal identification numbers, like our Social Security number, assigned to us to help distinguish us from other individuals. We may even consider our name to be part of our identity, and yet many of us have common names that we share with others. With these diverse definitions of identity available to us, it is interesting to note that when asked "what is your identity?" many people often respond with a quizzical look or a blank stare. Some will say something like "that depends," but the most profound answer and the one that seems most accurate is: "My identity is determined by a complex mix of things."

All people have an identity defined by their cultural classifications (nationality, race, religion and gender) as well as by societal characterizations (family, career, and position or title.) These are external components of identity that are bestowed upon them. Many people just use these labels or external definitions to describe their identity. However, there is value in going beyond these external descriptors to recognize one's total identity.

Internally, we also have natural gifts, strengths and capabilities. I call this your *"internal" identity*. This is the aspect of identity that needs to be nurtured and embraced. Awareness of your internal identity involves looking inside yourself and knowing what you know to be true about yourself, including your core values and beliefs.

The intellectual, emotional, physical and spiritual characteristics that comprise your uniqueness are all part of your identity. Your individual makeup goes beyond physical genetic characteristics and includes many aspects of your personality, such as your innate talents and abilities, your basic orientation toward the world around you, your learning styles, how you process and organize information, and other predisposed tendencies and characteristics. These are all part of your *internal* identity.

All of your sensory preferences – taste (what you like to eat), touch (what you like to touch and feel), smell (what pleases or displeases your olfactory senses), and sight (what you like in terms of color, shape, design or artistic motifs) – are uniquely ingrained in your identity. Even your religious and sexual preferences are part of your identifying features.

OUR SENSE OF IDENTITY

This relationship forms our IDENTITY

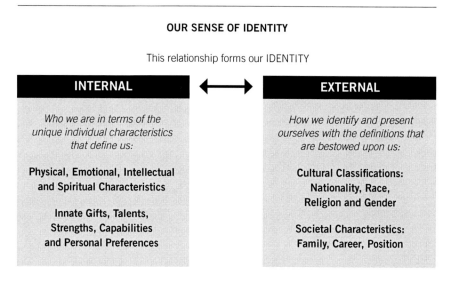

INTERNAL		EXTERNAL
Who we are in terms of the unique individual characteristics that define us:		*How we identify and present ourselves with the definitions that are bestowed upon us:*
Physical, Emotional, Intellectual and Spiritual Characteristics		**Cultural Classifications: Nationality, Race, Religion and Gender**
Innate Gifts, Talents, Strengths, Capabilities and Personal Preferences		**Societal Characteristics: Family, Career, Position**

This dynamic relationship is what makes our IDENTITY an evolutionary process.

Embracing your full identity requires accepting and supporting all its internal and external elements. Your gifts and strengths, your needs and challenges, your goals and dreams are all part of the fabric that is woven into the fiber of your being.

When your identity is formed from both components, you will be more apt to appreciate your uniqueness and the full sense of what makes you whole. The formation of your identity is an evolutionary process that balances the internal and external sources of that which defines who you are. Embracing both parts of your identity allows you to associate with others *and* to be uniquely individual. You are the totality of your cultural and societal classifications *together with* your distinctive physical, emotional, intellectual and spiritual characteristics.

As presented earlier, when your identity is formed from both sources, you have a foundation for who you "are" – not what you "do" or what you "have." When you embrace your whole identity, your motivation to achieve emanates from within.

With this awareness of your identity, striving to reach your potential comes from an internal motivation, and you are free to just *be*.

With full recognition of your *internal* identity – your internal truth – you are less likely to seek something else (connections, relationships, and/or accomplishments) to make you feel complete. Your identity can be thought of as who you are at your deepest core. The process of uncovering that core, and the ability to get in touch with who you are, is the first step toward living a sentient life.

Without awareness of our identity, we can not be authentic. How can we be "real" if we don't know what real is? Without knowledge of our values and core beliefs, how can we make decisions or know what we want? Our relationships, careers, lifestyle, and choices as an adult are all impacted by our identity. Awareness of our identity allows us to authentically choose our path in life.

Without knowledge of what makes our heart sing, what is important to us, or what is our life purpose, how can we form a vision for our future? Again, if we don't know who we are, how can we determine what we want and where we are going? The actions we take toward our vision must be consistent with our values, core beliefs and the essence of our identity if we are to be fulfilled and live our life to its highest purpose.

Awareness of your identity spawns your creativity, your passion, your energy and attraction, and your vision. That is YOU. It is empowering to tap into your internal gifts and talents. This self-knowledge helps you be on your power base. This is the central stance from which you draw your strength and stability. When you are on your power base, there is a solid foundation, and you are less likely to falter. To be fully sentient is to be empowered by living life from your power base. From this posture, you are in a better position to resist outside forces that threaten to move you off-center as you pursue fulfillment of your potential.

The development of our identity is an evolutionary process. For the most part, our genetic traits are predetermined characteristics that do not change throughout our life. However, since identity is a complex mix of our innate gifts, our predispositions, our hereditary personality characteristics, and the sum total of our experiences, it continues to develop over time as we grow and develop, expand our relationships, and have new experiences.

Our identity forms in relation to the concentric circles or *Relationship Circles of Influence* in our life. First, in early childhood, it is all about self. Our identity is central to our "world" which is defined by our basic needs and desires that are satisfied by our primary caregivers or immediate family. Eventually, as we develop,

RELATIONSHIP CIRCLES OF INFLUENCE

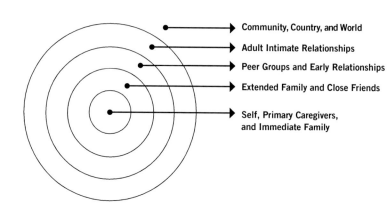

- Community, Country, and World
- Adult Intimate Relationships
- Peer Groups and Early Relationships
- Extended Family and Close Friends
- Self, Primary Caregivers, and Immediate Family

we expand that definition to include family values and lifestyle. Our lifestyle and identity are influenced by our heritage (including family values) and other external cultural factors. Once we begin interacting with playmates during the school years, peer relations add to our composite image of self. Teachers, extended family and other close friends also impact the formation of our identity or sense of self.

About the same time, environmental and social values creep into our personal definition of who we are. As we mature, societal influences have a more profound effect on our identity, especially in terms of our need for acceptance. So often, external acceptance takes precedence over self-acceptance as the yardstick by which we measure our value and worth. Eventually, intimate relationships have more influence on the formation of our identity than general social factors. Depending on our lifestyle and how we are raised, our community values may also affect our sense of identity. Even the definition of community becomes highly personal to each of us. Peer community, local community, our country, or the world are all prospective playing fields on which our personal identity develops and manifests itself.

Each moment of our past ultimately becomes part of our identity. The present is where our identity is expressed; by fully embracing our identity we can live authentically in the present. The future is impacted by our identity; our passions and our dreams form the goalposts on our playing field as we journey through life. The actions we choose each day carry us from the present moment toward our future aspirations. These actions, determined in part by our identity, serve as stepping stones to the future.

When does our sense of identity crystallize in our mind? Unfortunately, as human beings we rarely take the time to answer that question for ourselves. Instead, we often seek external validation of our identity. We search for different mechanisms to tell us who we are – astrology, tarot cards, personality tests, classes and work-shops, books, religion, and therapy are just some of the examples. Sometimes it is as if we are searching and wishing upon a star to define who we are.

We also avoid defining our true identity because of what I call the "Do Trap." As human beings we spend many years being praised for what we "do." As babies, we receive applause and cheers for each tiny achievement – rolling over, sitting up, crawling, standing, walking and going potty! In our formative years, we get rewarded with grades for what we do in school. We get athletic and academic commendations all the way through college for what we do. The do trap even extends to our adult years when the very first question most people ask when meeting someone is "What do you do?" It often seems as though it is not who we are but what we *do* that matters.

The "Do Trap" has two distant cousins: "Identity by association" and "Identity by possession." Many of us have been known at different times in our life as some-one's child, someone's spouse, and/or someone's parent. Who we are is relative to whom we are associated with, and we may even introduce ourselves that way! ("She's the President's daughter," or "That's the mother of the new American Idol," or "I'm John's wife.")

Some people are known by what they have or how much money they make – iden-tity in relation to possessions. These people may be classified by their homes, cars, country clubs, adult toys, and their bank accounts. ("He's the guy who drives the BMW and lives in that huge house on the corner," or "She's the lawyer who won the ten-million-dollar lawsuit," or "That's the couple who own the biggest boat on the river!")

When you have full awareness of your identity, you don't have to rely on external descriptors to define who you are. You get to be who you are – a unique being, accepted for your individual qualities and characteristics. With awareness and accep-tance of your internal identity, you are less likely to fall into the comparison trap; you are free to design your life for who you are, not for what others expect of you.

Each of us ought to know the answer to the question "What is my identity," but most of us have not taken the time to dig deep inside of ourselves for the true response. I invite you to learn about your own natural tendencies. There are many psychological instruments and personality inventories that are valuable tools for assessing personal orientation.

The acquisition of knowledge from these instruments can be helpful in understanding your genetic predisposition, learning style, emotional sensitivities, and other behavioral preferences. These instruments can be valuable in raising your consciousness because they can bring a deeper awareness of your natural preferences and orientations in multiple aspects of your life – home, career, relationships and personal growth. For example, how do you perceive or process information, organize your thoughts, and make decisions?

At the end of this chapter, there is a list of some well-known books, personality assessments and inventories that you may find helpful in your discovery process. I encourage you to gain expanded insight into your natural tendencies and innate qualities so that you may increase your communication, relationship, and decision-making effectiveness at work, at home and in life.

The secret to finding your identity, or internal truth, is solitude and silence. Rarely do busy beings choose to be quiet or alone. And yet, it is in the quietest of moments when you can look deep inside and discover your truth. The answers all lie within.

Finding your truth means really getting to know yourself. You can gain great insight and knowledge about yourself during peaceful moments of reflection, a quiet walk in nature, or through thoughtful contemplation while listening to quiet music. For some, personal awareness comes from exercising – jogging, biking, swimming, and other sports where you can be alone with your thoughts. Prayer and religious meditation can also yield inner knowledge. Still others of you may be able to gain insight and awareness by paying close attention to your dreams and the messages initiated in deep slumber.

As you grasp the full understanding of who you are, it is imperative that you compassionately love yourself in the process. No matter what you discover, you need to welcome that knowledge as your truth – the truth that makes you who you are. All people are miracles of life, unique beings unlike any one else. There may not be perfection in God's creation, but there is beauty in knowing that you were created as a distinctive being – a complex individual with a myriad of qualities that makes you whole.

With this discovery process, know that your authenticity, vision and actions all burst forth from the wellspring of your identity. Becoming one with your identity is an important first step toward becoming sentient and empowering yourself to reach your potential.

Discover Your Potential

The following questions are for your personal reflection as you seek to answer the question "What is my identity?"

- What traits are parts of my congenital make up?

- What parts of my identity have been assimilated through parental influence, religious norms or societal pressure?

- Which qualities describe my personality? What are my values and core beliefs?

- What are my preferences? What is important to me?

- What are my priorities in life?

- What are my natural talents and gifts?

- What challenges do I face? What comes naturally to me?

- What are my individual needs – in every sense of that word?

- What makes my heart sing?

- What causes me sadness and pain?

- What do I love about myself? What am I most proud of?

- What parts of myself do I embrace and cherish? What do I wish was different?

- To what degree do I accept myself as unique and unlike any other being?

- Am I able to see myself as God's blessing – a living miracle in this world?

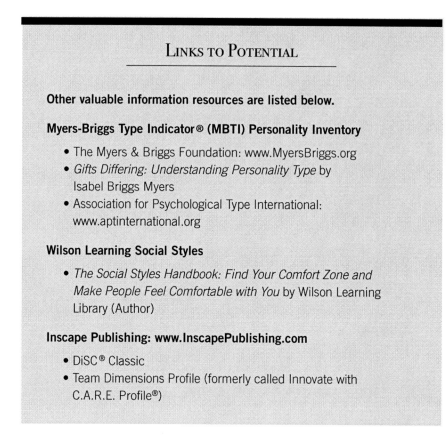

LINKS TO POTENTIAL

Other valuable information resources are listed below.

Myers-Briggs Type Indicator® (MBTI) Personality Inventory

- The Myers & Briggs Foundation: www.MyersBriggs.org
- *Gifts Differing: Understanding Personality Type* by Isabel Briggs Myers
- Association for Psychological Type International: www.aptinternational.org

Wilson Learning Social Styles

- *The Social Styles Handbook: Find Your Comfort Zone and Make People Feel Comfortable with You* by Wilson Learning Library (Author)

Inscape Publishing: www.InscapePublishing.com

- DiSC® Classic
- Team Dimensions Profile (formerly called Innovate with C.A.R.E. Profile®)

Core Values

Our core values are the ingrained beliefs and deepest ideals by which we live our life. Values are at the core of who we are as human beings. They are part of our identity. All of us have a set of values, beliefs, and meaningful philosophies to which we subscribe, consciously or unconsciously. In addition to individual values, there are different values that can be shared by a collective group or society including: ethical/moral, religious, political, social, familial and cultural. Values vary across people, organizations, communities and cultures.

Our values are shaped by three forces: Basic human emotional needs, individual genetic makeup, and personal experiences. These different aspects become ingrained into our being and form the foundation of our personal values. Our values evolve from different experiences with the external world as we grow and develop, form new relationships, and experience diverse groups, organizations and cultures. Thus, our values can change over time.

Individual experiences that affect personal values are varied. For the purposes of this discussion, the words environment and experience are used interchangeably. While your values appear innate and instinctive, they can change and evolve throughout your lifetime as you grow and develop. Your core values are influenced by many outside environmental forces, but your familial relationships (parental guidance and family philosophy) are not only the earliest influence on your value development but perhaps the strongest.

During your youth and throughout your formative years, education and religious upbringing continue to shape your values. Peer groups also have an impact on your values, and the degree to which peers are able to influence your values correlates with how well you are able to satisfy your basic emotional needs. A discussion of basic **Human Emotional Needs** follows in the next chapter.

Other societal influences including cultural and political pressures, as well as literature, media and advertising, are subtle but powerful factors in value formation. As people, we are impressionable and oftentimes receptive to waves of public opinion that change and evolve throughout our lifetime. Behavior that at one point in history is unacceptable or forbidden may become standard practice at a later time because political or environmental factors have influenced a change in mindset. This transformation in public thinking does not impact all individuals enough to change their values, but for some, public acceptance may be sufficient to reformulate part of their value system.

By the time you are an adult, your value system is pretty well ingrained in your personal makeup. However, different adult relationships can also have an impact on how you think and what you believe. Your individual values can be reshaped and reprioritized as part of your growth and development, demonstrated by the choices you make throughout your lifetime.

While our deepest core values are always important to each of us, sometimes we choose to disregard a value in favor of one that is more congruent with a special person in our life, such as a significant other. Groups, societies or cultures have values that are *generally* shared by their members. Sometimes, members will share a culture's values even if their personal values do not entirely agree with the normative values sanctioned by the collective group. This adaptation of values may have to do with their individual emotional needs, which are inextricably linked to their value system. Despite the common instances of adaptation of values, the *healthiest* of relationships and group associations have *real* congruency in their value systems.

CONTRIBUTING COMPONENTS OF CORE VALUES

Human Emotional Needs

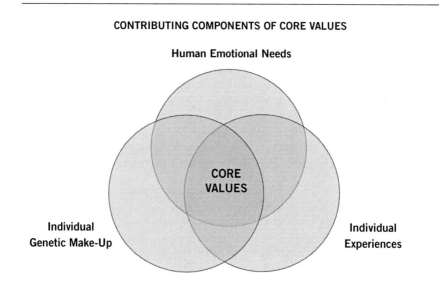

Individual Genetic Make-Up

CORE VALUES

Individual Experiences

Understanding your values is integral to embracing your identity and a critical first step in becoming authentic. Values affect how you live your life, form relationships, make decisions, and choose your actions. To become sentient and achieve your potential, you must live your life aligned with your values.

Awareness of your *personal* values will help you build stronger relationships in all parts of your life. Congruency of values is important with all personal interactions and associations such as: intimate/significant others, friends, neighbors, sports teams, and religious/social organizations. Values are part of your relationships with mentors, coaches, doctors, and service professionals whom you select to help you with your life. Similarity of values builds trust and cohesive relationships, helping to form a solid foundation from which they can grow. Alternatively, personal and business relationships that are *not* congruent with your personal values can have adverse emotional and physical consequences.

Values affect both how you spend your time and your motivation to pursue goals. They help you make better career decisions as you select the type of work you do and the organization in which you will work. Values influence your energy and motivation for accomplishment as well. You are more likely to be energized to prioritize your time and perform your responsibilities when you are aligned with your personal passion and values both at home and at work. As human beings, we are drawn to the activities, choices and people most closely aligned with our values.

Your values for work ethic, time management, quality, achievement, skill development, personal growth, communication, leadership, and organizational culture can influence the execution of your professional work and the results you achieve. If there is an incongruity of values between you and your manager, or with the organization itself, you may feel uncomfortable, unmotivated, insecure or even angry. In that situation, it would be difficult for you to do your best work, have pride in your performance, and/or reach your potential.

It is interesting to note that in recent decades, organizations have articulated and publicized their corporate values along with their mission and vision statements. In principle, this brings more humanity into the workplace and allows individuals to choose companies that align with their values. In practice, corporate values must be embraced and demonstrated at all levels of an organization for this principle to be effective. All employees must "walk the talk" of the corporate values and embody them in their relationship with others. If not, the corporate values are rendered meaningless within the context of a corporate culture, and some individuals may be negatively impacted by this transgression.

In summary, the alignment of values is critically important in all relationships whether they be with our family, friends, mentors, life partners or coworkers. Exploring and embracing our own values is the first step toward healthy relationships and congruent connections.

DISCOVERING YOUR CORE VALUES

By focusing on your core values, you'll begin the process of understanding your identity. The following awareness activities will help you discover and appreciate your values:

Stream of Consciousness
Clustering
Prioritizing

EXERCISES

EXERCISE 1: *Stream of Consciousness*

Find a time when you can be alone with your thoughts for a minimum of 30 minutes. Some people find it helpful to sit in their favorite chair or room of the house and put on soft inspirational music while they do this activity. Others may prefer to sit by a fireplace or, weather permitting, be outside with scenic natural elements. Ideally, you will find a comfortable place that will inspire personal meditation and free-flowing thoughts. You will need a journal to record your experience.

To begin, take a few deep breaths, close your eyes and feel the fresh air infuse your lungs and body with energy. Feel the vibrant pulsing of your heart, and concentrate on your deepest sensations. Take a few moments to be alone with your body, your energy and your thoughts.

When you are ready, begin writing all of the words that come to mind that represent your *values*. Ask yourself, what words have meaning for me for how I want to live my life? What values express the qualities I respect and strive for? What words describe important aspects of my identity, my relationships, my health, my work and my highest purpose?

There is no right or wrong answer here. Just let the words flow naturally onto your paper. Keep going until you can't think of any other words. When you reach that point, stop to take a few deep breaths with your eyes closed. Then review your list and see if more ideas spring forth from the words you have already created. Remember to think in terms of your whole being and your whole life. To help you, here are some sample questions that you might ask yourself as you do this exercise:

• What values are important to me?

• What values do I respect in others?

• What values were evident in my childhood?

• What did my parents value?

• What values do I want in my most significant relationship?

- What values would I want to teach my children?

- What do I value about my body, my home life, my work?

- What are the essential values for my spirituality?

- What do I value about community and my relationship to the world?

- What are my values concerning money and material possessions?

- What words would I use to describe my highest values impacting how I live my life?

To support you in this process, here are some sample words that people often think of as "values." Feel free to use any or all from this list in your journal. Allow these words to spark others for you as well.

Charity	Dedication	Health
Helping others	Honesty	Money
Gratitude	Integrity	Freedom
Creativity	Authenticity	Children
Commitment	Individuality	Friends and family
Spirituality	Love	Life Balance
Hard work	Affection	Trust
Perseverance	Generosity	Independence
Achievement	Loyalty	Joy and happiness

Remember, just let it flow! Enjoy the experience of breathing in new energy and letting ideas come forth naturally. Don't worry about the order of the words, just keep writing without regard for spelling, redundancy, or if two words mean similar things – just let it flow!

When you have completed this phase of the exercise, stand and stretch and take whatever time you need before you begin the process of "clustering" your values.

EXERCISE 2: *Clustering*

When you are ready, review your list of words that represent your values. Add, delete or change any that you want to at this time. Begin to see relationships between words, and put the words in groups that make sense to you. These "clusters" can be formed in any way that has meaning for you. There can be as many clusters as you want, and you may put as many words in a cluster as you desire. Words may be used in more than one grouping.

You most likely will have your own "cluster method;" choose the one that seems right for you. You may just begin putting words together that naturally seem to go together without having a definitive reason for pairing them. That's okay! When you have completed grouping the words together, feel free to label each cluster with a word that describes its particular category or why you have assembled those terms together.

When one woman did this exercise, she built a "tic-tac-toe" diagram and placed her words into the nine squares without understanding what the groupings meant at first. When she was done placing the words into their respective squares, she discovered that each grouping had a common theme, and she began labeling each square to represent its general meaning. She had a relationship group, a work/career group, a group that represented the values associated with what it means to "be an individual," and so on.

Two more examples of how others have clustered the value words:

• One individual divided her paper into wedges of a balance wheel representing eight segments of her life (Career, Money, Health, Spiritual and Personal Growth, Family and Friends, Personal Environment, Romance/Significant other, and Recreation/Hobbies). She then placed her value words into each section of the wheel that matched that area of her life. Certain values were important for her relationships, others for her career, some for her body and health, etc.

• Another individual just simply used an Excel spreadsheet and clustered the words in columns or "strings" that made sense. No labels, just lists of words that seemed to go together.

Have fun with the process of clustering your values. Discover what and how your values form parts of who you are and how they relate to your life. Enjoy this part of the process; play with the words and the natural associations between the words.

Again, there is no right or wrong answer. This exercise is meant to support your process of awareness. The more you think about and understand your values, the more you become one with your identity.

EXERCISE 3: *Prioritizing*

The last step of this process is to assess your different clusters and determine which ones are most important to you. First, prioritize the values in each cluster. Then prioritize the clusters in terms of importance for how you live your life. Is one cluster a natural precursor for another? If you could only pick one set of values, which one would it be? Are some clusters equal in their value or relation to your life?

Prioritizing is another way of becoming aware of your priorities, the things you value in your life. Your values and priorities are essential to your identity and ultimately to how you make decisions. Sometimes in life we must make decisions, and it can be difficult to choose one action over another. When we determine which course of action is consistent with our values, we are able to make better decisions. When our actions are aligned with our values, we are at our best!

Discover Your Potential

Our values are integral to all our decisions – our life choices, lifestyles, relationships and priorities. Once we have awareness of our values – true knowledge of that which is so important to us, we need to ask ourselves "Am I living consistently with my values?"

Below are some **Life Values Exercises** to help you examine if you are living consistently with your values. Take the time to do each exercise, and then evaluate how and if you might change your behavior to be more aligned with your value system.

- To see if your lifestyle choices are consistent with your values, look at your check book to see where and how you spend your money. What do you save, and what do you spend? What does your checkbook reveal about how you spend your time? What does your checkbook tell you about the activities and life experiences you value?

- Look at your family, friends, business associates/colleagues, and acquaintances, and evaluate who among your relationships most mirrors your values. Whose values are most different from yours? Does your analysis support the maxim that our healthiest relationships are with people who share our value system?

- Look back at all the places where you have worked or volunteered. Identify which positions were the most fulfilling and positive. Note the positions that felt negative, challenging, or caused you the greatest amount of stress. Then assess what were the values associated with each organization, manager, or work group with whom you worked. How did those values correlate with your positive/negative experiences with work?

- If you were given $1,000 to spend and told to take an imaginary shopping trip, how would you spend the money? What would you buy? Who would you buy for? What wouldn't you buy? Who wouldn't you buy for? Would you spend all of the money or save a part of it? What does this tell you about what is important to you at this time of your life?

- You just won the lottery. $1,000,000. Describe in detail how you would spend the money. Be sure to account for all the prize money which is *after* taxes!

- You were just told that you have, at the most, six months to live. How would you spend the rest of your life? In this exercise, money is not a factor in your decision. You hypothetically have all the money you need to do what you want. How and with whom would you spend your time? How would spirituality or religion fit into your life? Would you choose to work? If so, doing what? Would you be doing something different than you have ever done? If so, what would that be? Ask yourself "What is so important to me that I want it as part of my final months in this lifetime?"

Remember, your values are at the heart of your identity. Knowing your values and understanding the basic emotional needs and environmental experiences that shape your values are critical to living a life of fulfillment and achieving your potential. You now have a starting point – a baseline for understanding what you value in life. As you face decisions and choices on your journey, I recommend using the information that you have gained from these exercises to help navigate your personal road map to future goals.

I NEED

EMOTIONAL NEEDS

In his model, "Hierarchy of Needs," Abraham Maslow presents a foundational approach to understanding human motivation and behavior. In Maslow's model, an individual's physiological needs (air, water, food, shelter and bodily comforts) must be fulfilled first for survival. Maslow asserts that once we have physiological needs met, we then seek to satisfy our emotional needs. His original model delineates three primary sets of emotional needs including Safety and Security needs, Love and Belonging needs, and Esteem Needs. The Hierarchy of Needs model culminates with the need for self-actualization, which involves realizing potential, attaining fulfillment, and desire for personal growth.

In understanding how **Human Emotional Needs** relate to identity, values, and fulfillment of potential, the basic Human Emotional Needs model proposed by Dr. Todd Berntson is more useful for our discussion. Dr. Berntson's model is harmonious with Maslow's emotional needs categories, and it develops the analysis of human emotional needs to a slightly deeper level.

All individuals have a **Need for Identity**. Identity from this perspective simply means that a human being has a principal need to establish his own identity. In addition to the underlying need for identity, there are five basic emotional needs at the foundation of human behavior. They are:

> The need for connection
> The need to be effective
> The need to be valued
> The need for predictability
> The need for security

All of these needs are critical to our development and contribute to a healthy sense of identity. The degree to which a particular need is fulfilled will be reflected in the emotions elicited by the individual. These emotions are what motivate us to satisfy our basic needs.

THE NEED FOR CONNECTION

This is a basic human need for belonging and acceptance. Individuals do not live in isolation – they are not meant to be completely alone. Since prehistoric times, people have bonded within their groups, be it a tribe, commune, family or community. Survival of the individual was dependent on the cohesiveness of his/her group. So in the earliest of times, alienation from those upon whose support an individual depended usually meant death. Human beings are not well-equipped to live alone in nature. Modern medicine has proven that physical and emotional bonding with people, especially parents, is critical to the survival and development of infants. The need for connection transcends the purely physical and includes an emotional component that is necessary for survival. This need manifests itself as the drive for acceptance and the formation of relationships. The need for connection is not to be confused with the need for identity. Well-developed individuals balance their need for connection within the context of their identity. There is a healthy congruency between these two needs.

THE NEED TO BE EFFECTIVE

The need to be effective is about control of one's life. All people have the need to feel a certain sense of control – control of oneself and control over external events affecting their life. When this need is fulfilled, people feel empowered and energized. When this need is frustrated, people experience anxiety, helplessness and despair. This need affects people's ability to take responsibility for their life. A person has the option of feeling no control over his life – and hence, being a victim – or of being in absolute control of her life and being empowered.

THE NEED TO BE VALUED

The need to be valued is basic to the human condition. Esteem needs were among the first to appear on Maslow's Hierarchy of Needs and have long been evaluated as emotional drivers of behavior by other researchers. The need to be valued encompasses the need for self-esteem – to be acknowledged and valued by others. The level to which one feels valued contributes to one's sense of independence, status, achievement and overall well-being. Self-esteem is often associated with a sense of confidence. In this model, healthy self-esteem draws confidence from feeling accepted, appreciated and recognized as an individual.

THE NEED FOR PREDICTABILITY

The need for predictability is all about an individual's response to change. Nature endowed human beings with a need for stability and predictability. We need to know the rules of life! Routine and structure help individuals navigate through life without enduring the constant stress of being "on guard" or wondering "what will happen next." People will spontaneously create structure in their lives as a means of decreasing stress and becoming more efficient. The need for predictability is closely related to the need for effectiveness. Human beings often adapt to change more readily when they are in control of that shift of events. Without question, the need for predictability is also closely related to the need for security. Without predictability, security can neither be forecasted nor ensured. In today's world, where "change" is a constant, we see increased stress among individuals who require a strong sense of predictability.

THE NEED FOR SECURITY

Human beings have an innate need to feel safe, secure and protected; this is one of the most basic and essential human needs. Their survival depends on it. This concept is one of the most basic and essential needs that humans have. The need for security drives a basic orientation toward the outside world. Individuals need to assess whether their environment is supportive and safe. A sense of security is one of the elements driving every decision that an individual makes on a daily basis. With each new experience, people need to know how much risk is inherent in that situation. Conservative as well as risk-taking behaviors are driven by an individual's need for security.

Basic emotional needs are evident early in an individual's development. It appears that infants are born with a singular sense of identity – their world revolves around their basic needs. Infants elicit emotions to demonstrate their needs – crying when they are hungry or wet – until their *biological* needs are met. This correlates with Maslow's hierarchy of needs.

Since connection is one of the most basic human needs, it is understandable that as infants become aware of their surroundings and naturally bond with their primary caretakers, they elicit emotional responses, such as crying, when their basic emotional needs for *connection* and *security* are not met. This is substantiated through Erik Erikson's work on the Stages of Social-Emotional Development of Children. In 1956, he proposed that the first stage of development consists of the need for infants to develop basic trust and security. He stressed that these emotional needs of being loved and nurtured are critical to healthy development.

Young children also have a need to be *effective*. As small children become more capable and able to do things by themselves or participate in household chores, they exhibit heartfelt emotions to show how proud they are of their accomplishments. Knowing that they can fulfill a parent's request to do something ("Put these napkins on the dinner table" or "go put your shoes by the door") empowers toddlers and reinforces their feelings of being helpful and being effective members of the family. On the other hand, the same child who effectively follows a parent's request to put his shoes by the door may feel frustrated, and hence ineffective, when trying unsuccessfully to tie his shoes by himself.

Conversely, we see different emotions (anger, disappointment or frustration) elicited if the child doesn't get what he or she wants (for example when a parent says "no"). As children develop, this same type of emotional response, correlating with the need to be effective, shows up when toddlers are playing with other children and can't have the toy they want. They can become upset or frustrated when they do not feel effective in getting what they want.

Learning autonomy and initiative are the next two stages of development in children. These stages reveal a child's need to be *effective* as her identity expands.

Jumping ahead to view "the rebellious teenage years," oftentimes teens will strive to have their own identity by resisting family or cultural "norms." It is not uncommon for teenagers to break or bend the family rules by staying out past curfew or going somewhere that is forbidden. The teenage girl who sneaks make-up into her school bag to put on *after* she leaves home in the morning is another instance of a youngster's quest for independence and a separate identity.

A more extreme example of teenagers rebelling as they search for identity would be the teens who dress uniquely with outrageous clothes, colored or shaved hair, extensive piercings, and so on. This example merely demonstrates the natural need humans have to define their individual identity. This is consistent with Erikson's fifth stage of emotional development in which learning identity is a major focus of the adolescent's development. Erikson suggests that teens will experiment with different roles to answer the question "Who am I?" and even the most well-adjusted adolescents may dabble with rebellion as a form of distinguishing their own identity.

Throughout our life, the fulfillment of our emotional needs influences our overall well-being. Research on human social and emotional development indicates that when basic emotional needs are not met in childhood, adults suffer negative consequences in their lives. This carryover of unmet needs impacts relationships at home and at work. People may be in relationships or jobs where they feel disappointed, frustrated or unsatisfied. A closer look at these situations might reveal that their individual emotional needs are not being met. In actuality, they may be feeling unconnected, ineffective, or not valued in these relationships or positions. Positive and negative feelings, associated with the fulfillment of our emotional needs, are prevalent all through life.

A discussion of the human need for identity brings us full circle to a basic proposition of this book. You need to know who you are to become sentient, achieve fulfillment and realize your potential. Many of the exercises in this book highlight the need to define your own identity from an *internal* perspective. Identity is about embracing who you are, including understanding your emotional needs.

To be authentic you need to embrace your distinct identity. When individuals seek external definition or validation of their identity, they are less empowered. Externally focused identity can lead to external conformity. External conformity is the enemy of self-awareness and self-acceptance for, at its extreme, it necessitates the denial of one's own true identity and submission to the authority of an institution or public opinion. Excessive conformity leads to a complete detachment from personal identity. In this condition, people act in ways that they deem to be socially acceptable and, in doing so, denounce their individual identity.

> **To be authentic you need to embrace your distinct identity.**

Awareness of what makes you unique and what fulfills your emotional needs is what will offer you the greatest self-acceptance and personal power. Knowledge of your own identity and individuality translates to self-acceptance, value and self-worth.

Additionally, not only is your behavior impacted by your basic human emotional needs, but your values are as well. Therefore, understanding your underlying needs is often helpful in examining your values and life choices. Self-assessment of your emotional needs can help you better understand current behaviors that affect your relationships, work, and other life choices. Adults don't often thoroughly examine their human emotional needs. Without awareness of their emotional needs, they have an incomplete assessment of their identity and, therefore, may end up less likely to achieve their goals or full potential.

Most importantly, an understanding of your emotional needs can both offer you clarity on why past relationships or jobs didn't *feel right* or work out and enhance your ability to make better decisions now and in the future. When you are able to assess how well your needs are being met *and* if you are able to successfully communicate those feelings with others, you are more likely to improve personal and business relationships as you move forward with your life.

DISCOVERING YOUR EMOTIONAL NEEDS

Using Dr. Berntson's model of the five basic **Human Emotional Needs**, each need can be expressed as an emotion on a continuum of feeling. Depending on individual needs, how a person feels and the expression of that feeling will fall some-where in the range of emotions that are correlated with the basic human needs:

HUMAN EMOTIONAL NEEDS

Connection	Alienated •ıı• Engaged
Effectiveness	Anxious •ıı• Empowered
Valued	Rejected •ıı• Esteemed
Predictability	Stressed •ıı• Confident
Security	Fearful •ııı• Nurtured

It is important to note that "insecurity" can be experienced in all five dimensions when the emotional need is not met. "Confidence" has more to do with predict-ability of outcome than positive self-esteem in this model. Individuals can lack confidence when they can't *trust*. Further, be careful of semantics, in that, in the course of this discussion words like insecurity and confidence may be used to denote different meanings.

Emotional needs are met from the outside in. If you want to feel better about your inner self, you must first create circumstances in the world around you that feed you emotionally. Each of the basic emotional needs is critical to your healthy development and survival.

At a subconscious level, people elicit emotions to motivate themselves to satisfy their underlying needs. It is impossible to have emotional needs met over the long term without an external support system. Even with positive self-esteem and personal confidence, if individuals exist in an environment that undermines their emotional needs, they will soon become stressed or even depressed.

People make decisions based on needs, perceptions and emotions that are not always within their conscious level of understanding. Sometimes people make decisions that just "feel" right to them, and in doing so they are responding at an unconscious level to a basic emotional need. As human beings, we all have these basic emotional needs. Our individuality stems from the degree to which we have these distinct needs. Our values, our choices and our actions are all representa-tive of our needs.

There are also ways to compensate for lack of fulfillment of needs from a particu-lar situation. To illustrate this point, a woman, 15 years into her career, was in a new position where she felt frustrated and unhappy about her work. She felt no connection to the organization, and she was not utilizing her best innate talents in the course of her daily responsibilities. She did not feel effective or valued as a result. By the very nature of the economic climate – there were few jobs available and lots of organizational layoffs – she had a high degree of insecurity. Her company continuously made changes to management, structure, and compensation of its employees, which resulted in a sense of unpredictably.

With the uncertainty of an impending layoff, she felt anxious and unprepared for what each day might bring. She did not know how to handle the situation – a clear example of unfulfilled emotional needs – when she was unprepared to seek another position for full-time employment. She felt "trapped" in the job because she did not believe she had choices.

With coaching, she made the decision to stay in the job while pursuing other creative and professional interests. She worked nights and weekends to develop a side business using her talents and skills in pursuits that she loved. She still experienced some feelings associated with fear of being laid off, insecurity about the loss of a consistent paycheck, but on a day-to-day basis, she nurtured her creativity, structured her time so that she felt more effective and productive, and she systematically planned for unemployment by building a foundation for her own business. By the time she was laid off, which happened quite unexpectedly and forcefully six months later, she had a strong sense of how to build a business that would allow her to feel empowered, valued, and of service to others.

Perhaps you can identify with her situation, the feelings she endured, and the difficult choice she needed to make as she balanced the unrewarding job situation with her insecurity and her fear of loss of employment and a paycheck. In the end, although she had worked long hours, nights and weekends, she was able to see what she had gained – an opportunity to pursue her passion, more personal fulfillment, and a stronger sense of security and control over her own destiny.

While the assessment of how our emotional needs are satisfied is directly linked to *external* circumstances and social relationships, we are in a position to have a fulfilling emotional relationship with ourself when we have a comprehensive awareness of self. We all have the ability to embrace our values, natural gifts and strengths. There is a sense of fulfillment in connecting with ourself, valuing who we are (identity), and knowing what qualities and innate talents make us effective as we live our lives.

When we connect with and value ourselves, we feel empowered and have greater security and control in relation to the changes that impact our lives. This core relationship with self signifies that we honor who we are by embracing our authentic being. In doing so, we develop a standard against which we can measure external social relationships, and we are in a better position to recognize when our emotional needs are being met.

You need to embrace your innate talents and the skills that you have gained from your life's experiences. If you recognize your gifts and believe you have something of value to offer others, you are likely to be more effective in building relationships and meeting your goals.

Ideally, you want to feel an internal sense of well-being at your core. When you know who you are, know what you want, and are able to appreciate emotional fulfillment from within, then life situations and social relationships can be measured against how you feel about yourself. If you feel whole and empowered by your own sense of self, you can remain centered in your encounters with other people in your life. When you honor yourself, and remain true to your expectations for emotional fulfillment, the best jobs, relationships, and social opportunities will converge into a unified, integrated life.

EXERCISES

EXERCISE 1: *Emotional Needs Self Test*

Using the following emotional needs self-test, you will begin the process of understanding the condition of your human emotional needs. For each of the five basic needs described below, select a position on the continuum that best describes *how you feel most of the time*. Circle the number that correlates with your feeling.

Connection	Alienated	1	2	3	4	5	6	7	8	9	10	Engaged
Effectiveness	Anxious	1	2	3	4	5	6	7	8	9	10	Empowered
Valued	Rejected	1	2	3	4	5	6	7	8	9	10	Esteemed
Predictability	Stressed	1	2	3	4	5	6	7	8	9	10	Confident
Security	Fearful	1	2	3	4	5	6	7	8	9	10	Nurtured

Emotional Needs Assessment Scores: (1-10)

Which number best correlates with how you feel?

Connection _____ Effectiveness _____ Valued _____

Predictability _____ Security _____

This Emotional Needs self-test simply measures *how you see yourself* in relation to your world. It is representative of how you feel at this time, even though your responses may change at different points of your life. Recognize that there is no right or wrong answer here; this self-test is simply mirroring your emotional response to these questions at this moment in your life.

It may also be helpful to take this self-assessment as a measure of different aspects of your life. People have used this tool to evaluate whether or not a current position is serving their overall well-being. Others have tested their impression of how their needs will be met in a prospective job. The same test may be applied in evaluating significant relationships.

EXERCISE 2: *Situational Exercises*

Use the following scales to evaluate your emotional needs satisfaction related to your career and relationships.

Career or Job Assessment

Connection	Alienated	1	2	3	4	5	6	7	8	9	10	Engaged
Effectiveness	Anxious	1	2	3	4	5	6	7	8	9	10	Empowered
Valued	Rejected	1	2	3	4	5	6	7	8	9	10	Esteemed
Predictability	Stressed	1	2	3	4	5	6	7	8	9	10	Confident
Security	Fearful	1	2	3	4	5	6	7	8	9	10	Nurtured

Career Emotional Needs Assessment Scores: (1-10)
Which number best correlates with how you feel?

Connection _____   Effectiveness _____   Valued _____

Predictability _____   Security _____

Relationship Assessment

Connection	Alienated	1	2	3	4	5	6	7	8	9	10	Engaged
Effectiveness	Anxious	1	2	3	4	5	6	7	8	9	10	Empowered
Valued	Rejected	1	2	3	4	5	6	7	8	9	10	Esteemed
Predictability	Stressed	1	2	3	4	5	6	7	8	9	10	Confident
Security	Fearful	1	2	3	4	5	6	7	8	9	10	Nurtured

Relationship Emotional Needs Assessment Scores: (1-10)
Which number best correlates with how you feel?

Connection _____   Effectiveness _____   Valued _____

Predictability _____   Security _____

While all of us have these five basic emotional needs, most likely one of them will prove to be the *primary* emotional need that motivates our behavior. In the previous chapter, you discovered, evaluated and prioritized your values. Now that you have a baseline reading on your emotional needs, you can explore the connection between your values and emotional needs. This process will highlight which one or two emotional needs surface as your *primary* emotional need(s). This exercise may help create awareness of the reasons you value the things you do. It can also be revealing and helpful in understanding personal motivation for the choices and decisions you make.

> Emotional needs are directly linked to life fulfillment. They are also closely related to personal values. Understanding this correlation facilitates your ability to achieve fulfillment and your potential.

CORE VALUES AS RELATED TO EMOTIONAL NEEDS
You can further understand your values by evaluating what emotion underscores the importance of that value in your life. Each of your values can be correlated with a primary and secondary emotional need to explain its significance.

The same value may have different needs underlying its existence for two different people. For example, two individuals may list **Money** as something they value. For one person, money may be an expression of his or her **need to feel safe and secure**. He or she may also value money because its existence supports the **need for predictability**. Another person may value money because it allows him or her to feel empowered, *and* it fulfills the need for "status" which supports externally focused identity.

EXERCISE 3: *Values and Needs Analysis*

In this exercise, you will link your values to your primary emotional needs. Reflect back to the values exercises completed earlier in this book and, in the chart below, list your top ten values in the left-hand column. Then select a corresponding emotional need that you believe each value represents to you. Choose from the basic five emotional needs of: connection, effectiveness, value, predictability and security.

Ask yourself "What drives my need for this value?" As suggested in the sample below, for each value select a primary and secondary emotional need that seems associated with it. Remember, the same value may have different needs associated with it for different people. The correlation of a value to an emotional need depends on the connotation and meaning of that value in a person's life. Again, there is no right or wrong answer, just another measure for gaining awareness of your values and needs.

Example: top ten values related to emotional needs for Sue Johnson.

Top Ten Values	Primary Emotion Need	Secondary Emotional Need
1) Achievement	Valued	Effectiveness
2) Honesty	Predictability	Connection
3) Freedom	Security	Effectiveness
4) Independence	Security	Predictability
5) Family	Connection	Security
6) Love	Connection	Valued
7) Commitment	Connection	Valued
8) Communication	Effectiveness	Connection
9) Respect	Connection	Valued
10) Trust	Connection	Security

Now it is your turn to create your top ten values related to your Emotional Needs:

Top Ten Values	Primary Emotional Need	Secondary Emotional Need
Sample: Achievement	Valued	Effectiveness
1)		
2)		
3)		
4)		
5)		
6)		
7)		
8)		
9)		
10)		

Once you have listed your top ten values in the left column and chosen a primary and secondary need that is associated with that value, review your responses to be sure that they accurately reflect why each value is important to you.

EXERCISE 4: *Determining You Primary Emotional Need*

From the information listed in the sample table for Sue Johnson (Exercise #3), the following grid lists the number of times that an emotional need shows up as a Primary Need and a Secondary Need for Sue's values. Notice that there can only be 10 primary and 10 secondary needs listed. The right hand column tallies the total number of times each emotional need is listed as either a primary or secondary need for Sue's top ten values.

Emotional Needs	# Times Primary	# Times Secondary	# Times Total
Connection	5	2	7
Effectiveness	1	2	3
Valued	1	3	4
Predictability	1	1	2
Security	2	2	4
TOTAL	10	10	20

Notice that the emotional need that appears most often for Sue is **Connection** with seven appearances. The need to be **Valued** and the need for **Security** each show up four times in her listing. However, **Security** is listed twice as a primary need and **Valued** only once as a primary need, so although they both total four times, her need for **Security** is slightly stronger than her need to be **Valued**.

Using your information from Exercise #3 where you listed your top ten values related to emotional needs, in the table below, count up the number of times each of the five basic emotional needs appears in your list. Count both places that a need appears on your list as a primary need and/or secondary need. Record your totals in the table below:

Emotional Needs	# Times Primary	# Times Secondary	# Times Total
Connection			
Effectiveness			
Valued			
Predictability			
Security			
TOTAL			

Which basic emotional need appears most often on your values analysis? Which emotional need appears least often? Are two or more of the emotional needs equal in the number of times they are associated with your top ten values? Are there any that do not appear at all?

Now, prioritize your five emotional needs in a final list, in order of the overall frequency each appears in your values analysis. (Note, if two needs have the same total number of appearances in your analysis, prioritize them in terms of which one shows up more often as a primary need.) Remember that two or more needs may sometimes have the same frequency in this exercise for some individuals.

Example: Primary Emotional Need   *Connection*_____

My Primary Emotional Need: _____

My Secondary Emotional Need: _____

Third: _____

Fourth: _____

Fifth: _____

The assumption behind this exercise is that the things we value will usually be feeding the emotional need that is most important to us or the one that is least fulfilled and, therefore, most insecure. Now that you have completed this exercise, ask yourself: *How well does this self-test represent which of my emotional needs are currently satisfied? How do my emotional needs affect my relationships at home, at work and in life? Which emotional needs would I like to reinforce so that I can strengthen my confidence and live life from my power base?*

DISCOVER YOUR POTENTIAL

To continue the process of discovery, I encourage you to journal your thoughts as you reflect on what you have learned about your **Emotional Needs**. You might also ask yourself the following questions to deepen your learning:

- How do I view my world – is it nurturing or dangerous?

- Do I generally feel connected to others or alone?

- When do I feel most connected and engaged with others?

- When do I feel most valued and esteemed?

- Do I have a sense of control over my life?

- What circumstances in my life are beyond my control?

- Do I feel blessed or do I see myself as a victim?

- Do I feel cherished and respected, or do I feel worthless?

- Do I see change as positive or negative?

- Do I flow with change, or am I easily stressed when life becomes unpredictable?

Links to Potential

Other valuable information resources are listed below.

- Abraham H. Maslow: www.Maslow.com

- Dr. Todd Berntson: www.DrTodd.com

AUTHENTICITY

Authenticity means that "I act according to who I am. I am one with and express my identity. Therefore, I acknowledge my individuality and the uniqueness of my being – even if that means I am separate and apart from others. I accept that I am unique, and I accept others for their separateness and individuality in all parts of my life."

Authenticity is the outward projection of your identity. It is what you project. It is how you live your life in accordance with your values and your truth. In its purest sense, authenticity means not changing the real you to make someone like you or to be accepted by others.

The opposite of living authentically is assimilation (also referred to as conformity). By definition, assimilation means the state of being assimilated. This definition highlights that conformity takes place when a person or minority group, for example, gradually adopts the customs and attitudes of a prevailing culture. If authenticity is more desirous, let's explore why people may assimilate instead of remaining true to their identity.

The reasons for assimilation may be twofold. People may choose to conform so that they will be accepted. They may choose a form of assimilation to avoid suffering the potentially negative consequences of being different if their values, beliefs or personal preferences are different from others. This most often happens when the individual's emotional needs are not met, and they rely on external sources for self-definition and acceptance. As stated earlier, excessive conformity leads to a complete detachment from personal identity.

Conformity may also be imposed on people and, therefore, it is coerced, not chosen. A case in point is cultural conformity that is expected by the majority. Religious and racial groups have most often felt the sting of this kind of forced assimilation. Even in America, historically people have been expected to speak English to communicate regardless of their country of origin, which is representative of a cultural undertone of expected assimilation. Total conformity, for the most part, does not exist in our country. The current trend, with our global marketplace, celebrates diversity as we strive to embrace differences and recognize the value of individuals.

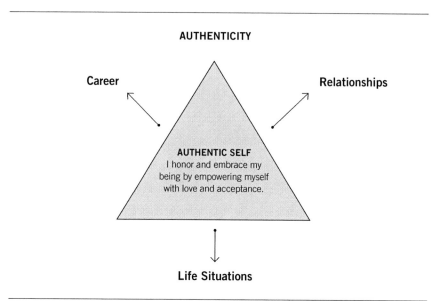

However, we all assimilate (or conform), to some degree, at different times in order to be a part of a larger system. In a diverse environment like the United States, assimilation may be necessary in order to preserve economic survival. People may need to adjust language and lifestyle practices in order to secure a job and a safe place to live for their families. As long as core values and beliefs are not sacrificed, assimilation may be necessary for survival and, therefore, acceptable.

In an idealistic world, individuals would always be free to be who they are (consistent with their values and beliefs) without fear of rejection or consequences. There would be no expectation of assimilation or conformity. True diversity would be appreciated, the world would be richer, and human differences would be celebrated and valued. Being authentic would be consistently rewarded, regardless of the presence of divergent viewpoints.

In the real world, complete with political, economic and social pressures, however, people are not always able to sustain the purest form of authenticity at all times. When individuals are not authentic, they may experience negative consequences that impact their health and well-being. So the question remains, how can you hold firm to your authentic self while coexisting in a world with expectations and group pressures? The answer lies somewhere between conformity and compromise.

If conformity means that an individual has to deny his core values and beliefs in order to exist within a group or an organization, then his authenticity is diminished or eradicated. If, however, in order to succeed in a society, community or organization, individuals adjust their behavior to be accepted (or to achieve personal goals) while keeping their core values intact, then their authenticity is not sacrificed.

In business today, it is necessary to conform to organizational norms, beliefs, ideologies and social practices in order to be accepted, be evaluated as "effective" and/or advance to a desired position. Often there is a great deal of pressure to conform, and the consequences for not adhering to expected practices may result in loss of employment. Some feel that conformity is a form of "selling out" because it may involve denouncing one's preferences (or values) in lieu of the corporate norm, which is akin to "selling your soul."

There are a few things to consider in relation to authenticity and assimilation if you are working in today's business community: First, there are modifications that all individuals need to make in order to "fit in" or adjust to different corporate cultures. Usually these changes pertain to behaviors rather than beliefs. The extent to which a person conforms is an individual choice and one that must be made in alignment with his or her core values. These are the choices people make every day in their employment. As long as these choices don't contradict your core values, then you can still be authentic. You need to always trust your internal truth even in the midst of accepting or participating in alternative behavior.

Also, when you are in a position or in an organization that does not support your authenticity – one that is not aligned with your values, you create the potential for great internal emotional and physical suffering that results from the incongruity between your behavior and your values.

One of my clients found herself in a position that did not match her personal ideology. She compromised her belief system because the position paid well, but at the time she did not recognize how the situation was taking its toll on her health and well-being. Her job falsely met her emotional need for security, but it did not feed her emotional need to feel effective, valued and engaged as her authentic self. She ultimately felt emotionally depleted and physically ill. She stayed in her job at severe personal cost.

Another man, who was extremely creative and free-spirited, with a generous habit of helping others outside of his regular responsibilities, was in a position reporting to the president who had a very different style than he. More importantly, the president's values were dissimilar from his. She was authoritative and demanding; he was engaging and supportive to his direct reports. In order to conform to her performance mandates and behavioral expectations, he had to give up his natural approach. He was expected to do his job exactly as she prescribed. This left no room for creativity, and it was not aligned with his most effective communication and performance style.

He had a choice: to conform to his manager's rules of conduct and hold his employees accountable to her expectations or to lose his job. His decision was easy – he was true to himself and made the decision to leave the company and find a position that allowed him to be authentic. He did not want to work in an organization that expected conformity to a singular authority, nor did he want to spend his time in an environment where he could not utilize his talents to empower others and achieve his best results.

Perhaps you have found yourself in a challenging situation that resembles either of these two examples. Or you may be wondering how to avoid this type of situation in the future. The answer is to choose an organization that *fits your values* or one that celebrates diversity (including diversity of cultures, lifestyles and thought) so that you don't have to compromise to be accepted. Adapting to a new or different culture, while expected, should not require you to compromise your sense of identity or core values. Choosing to be authentic, in some circumstances, can be difficult. Making the choices necessary to achieve your goals and succeed in all of these situations requires self-esteem and confidence.

Discover Your Potential

Questions for reflection:

- When do I feel most authentic and free to be myself?

- When has it been difficult for me to be authentic?

- How have I balanced the need to assimilate in an organization with the need to be authentic?

- When have I not been authentic or true to my own values and needs; what happened?

- In which area of my life do I want to enhance my ability to be authentic?

CONFIDENCE

Both confidence and authenticity are linked to the successful fulfillment of basic emotional needs. When individuals feel engaged with others, empowered, secure and able to "flow" with change, their self-esteem can be developed from within. With a strong self-esteem, they live life from their power base and are more capable of being authentic.

To possess real confidence, people must draw their self-esteem from within. Sometimes people wrongly assume that others can "give" them their self esteem. They seek an external definition and affirmation of who they are. If this were true, then positive self-esteem would be just as easily withdrawn, when the individual faced disapproval from others. No one else can "make" a person feel confident or secure in his identity – this is solely the responsibility of the individual. Other people can "shake" another person's confidence when it is not well-established and drawn from within.

It is often surprising which individuals suffer from lack of confidence. Looking from the outside in, a person may appear to "have it all:" intelligence, good looks, athletic prowess, and the ability to achieve their desired goals. But inside themselves, they may not see or believe what others do.

For example, when we reflect on the legendary lives and tragic deaths of luminaries such as actress Marilyn Monroe, writer Ernest Hemingway and his beautiful granddaughter actress Margaux Hemingway, artist Vincent Van Gogh, and British novelist Virginia Woolf – all people with extraordinary gifts – we can't help but speculate that they might have suffered from a lack of healthy self-esteem.

> Confidence is all about the messages that we send to ourselves. These messages affirm that which makes us unique: our values, gifts, needs, challenges and goals. Confidence ultimately comes from knowing and trusting our inner truth.

A person's lack of confidence can be a mystery to those who do not understand the phenomenon of how self-esteem is developed. Self-esteem comes from embracing your natural talents and gifts. Confidence builds from the inside out. For some, gaining confidence takes conscious effort and attention to the concept "we are what we think." Confidence is really just an attitude, and it comes from believing in yourself and embracing the knowledge that you are an individual miracle.

Real confidence is derived from a clear sense of identity together with the fulfillment of our individual emotional needs. Confidence is all about the messages that we send to ourselves – the messages that affirm that which makes us unique – our values, gifts, needs, challenges and goals. Confidence ultimately comes from knowing our inner truth and trusting that truth.

The process of acknowledging our truth is what I call *Coaching to the Core*, a process of internal self-coaching or "coaching for confidence." This self-guided coaching involves building positive messages that are designed to reinforce your basic emotional needs. It is a process of self-nurturing.

COACHING TO THE CORE
There are two parts to this self-coaching process. The first part involves understanding your **core beliefs** and identifying those beliefs that serve you well and those that limit you. A core belief is one that is so basic to the way you think that oftentimes it is disregarded as conscious thought – a thought that can be changed if it does not serve you well. Your core beliefs, much like your values, are integrally related to your basic emotional needs and are formed from multiple sources throughout your lifetime.

During our childhood and formative years, our belief system is closely tied to our parents, early education and religious doctrines. Throughout our lifetime, however, our internal belief system is continuously restructured by close relationships, friends, colleagues, community, and the media. As adults we hold onto many beliefs that ultimately influence our behavior, choices and decisions.

Consciously we don't always recognize these beliefs as core influencers of our life, nor do we separate those beliefs that serve us well and those that interfere with our ability to be our best. There are dozens of messages that inundate us every day that have the power to influence our self-concept *if we let them*.

There are a lot of examples of the positive messages many of us hear: "You can be anything you want to be!" "I know you will be a success, no matter what you decide to do." "You're so smart; I know you will achieve great things!" "You are beautiful; you can have anyone you want!" "I wish I looked like you." "You are so nice, generous and kind; people will love you wherever you go." "You're good in math – you should be a scientist or an engineer." "You write so well." "You are so artistic and talented." The list could go on and on. For all of us, there are lots of messages that reinforce our natural talents and personality characteristics, as do the opinions of other people like our family, friends and well-meaning teachers.

Conversely, many of us are subjected to negative messages that come from different sources including parents, peers, teachers, and the powerful influences of advertising and media. The examples that come to mind include: "You are not good enough – you will never amount to anything!" "You are not living up to your potential." "What is wrong with you? Can't you do anything right?" "You eat so much you are going to get fat!" "No one will listen to you – you're nobody." "You can't change the world – you have no control over what happens."

We all know the generic messages about life that come from media and society. There are messages that suggest you need to have white teeth, the perfect body, or the right clothes to be attractive. Other messages arise from gender (or racial, religious, or cultural) bias such as: *Girls aren't as strong and tough as boys. Men should wear the pants in the family. Women can't be as successful as men in business. A pretty woman won't be taken seriously at work. It's a man's world! Real men dress a certain way and drink a certain beer!*

The list of the messages we hear throughout our lifetime is highly personal to each of us. You may have heard some of the positive or negative messages described above. While we are all continuously subjected to a multitude of messages, each of us selectively (and perhaps unconsciously) holds onto certain messages as the prevailing beliefs that guide our actions and our life.

Although core beliefs flow into your subconscious from a myriad of sources, when you consciously accept a belief as truth, it becomes your own – for better or worse. What you do with these messages, once they are internalized, is what ultimately influences your self-confidence. The positive messages will continue to reinforce your self-image and support your emotional needs, but negative messages can conflict with your self-worth and personal goals if you let them. Negative messages can limit your capacity to thrive, so these messages are called *limiting beliefs*.

RAISING CONSCIOUSNESS

As a first step in developing greater confidence, I encourage you to examine the messages that you have internalized and raise them to a conscious level. The goal is to emphasize internal positive messages and build your sense of core confidence from inside yourself. Harmful negative messages may have stigmatized you or limited your ability to live to your fullest potential in the past. While it is not realistic to expect that you can change all your beliefs ingrained since early childhood, it is possible to raise your consciousness about the kinds of internal messages you want to accept and reinforce for yourself.

Coaching to the Core involves evaluating which external messages you have captured and made a part of your self-talk. You may know *self-talk* as that little voice inside you. I like to think of it as "mind chatter." To have a sense of self-assurance we need to nurture ourselves with positive self-talk. Just as if we were talking to a loved one or best friend, we need to encourage ourselves with self-directed messages to fill emotional voids and create a greater sense of self-reliance.

So often, individuals use the negative messages that they hear while growing up to self-deprecate and diminish their own well-being. As adults, if you want to grow, develop, and achieve your dreams, you must decide which messages will fortify your own mind. You need to ask yourself "which message matters?" and then decide to disregard the messages that feed self-doubt. You have the power to decide what you want to believe! This core coaching exercise is simply a way to feel good about yourself. It is about energizing yourself with loving messages that affirm your special qualities.

Our feelings are closely linked to our thoughts. Some would argue that it is not possible to change how we feel. Others would say that we cannot change how a person feels but that our thoughts are powerful stimulators of emotion. Thought is a powerful instrument that metaphysically can shape your reality. In a way, life is a mind game, and you play it with yourself! So then – play to win! Be your own compassionate coach, and support yourself with the mind messages you really want to hear.

Exploring your core beliefs in the process of awareness is critical to personal growth and development. Taking ingrained core beliefs and raising them to a conscious level will allow you to understand their impact on your thinking and behavior. Think of core beliefs as "old friends" that are akin to an old pair of slippers that feel so comfortable and good. Some beliefs just feel natural and are accepted as reality from the habitual practice of believing them. When a belief is self-limiting, we must reprogram ourselves to raise our consciousness and develop a new thought to replace the one that doesn't serve us well.

Raising awareness of your core beliefs exposes the emotional needs clinging to your unconscious thoughts. This exploration requires energy for growth, but it can also be *energizing*. What you will discover is that self-awareness and learning are invigorating! It is empowering to make decisions and to do things on purpose – even changing your thoughts. This process of intellectual growth is what *Coaching to the Core* is all about – learning new patterns of thought and making conscious choices.

Developing new thoughts and creating affirmations require dedicated thought and daily commitment to embed them at a deeper level. This process is much like developing a new habit – practice makes perfect. The reward for developing positive self-talk is definitely worth the effort. When an individual relies on internal sources of strength and identity, she is better able to handle external circumstances that impact daily living, and there is greater opportunity for growth.

Shifting your limiting beliefs to positive thoughts requires believing in what is possible as well as developing new mind messages. But first, you will need to actively interfere and STOP the old negative chatter that automatically creeps into your conscious mind. You do this by using a technique adapted from neurolinguistic programming (NLP).

Whenever you experience a limiting belief or an undesirable emotion, like anger, you need to break the automatic response pattern by creating a new link between your other-than-conscious and conscious mind. The method engages both the right brain (creative) and left brain (logical) to create an opportunity for your conscious mind to purposefully send messages to the subconscious. This process has four simple steps:

1. Create a STOP button for yourself – a quick and decisive movement that signifies outwardly that you want to stop something. Shouting the word "Stop," or slapping your hand emphatically on your chest, or clapping your hands loudly as you say "Stop" are all variations on personal "stop buttons."

2. Then take a deep breath and release the air slowly.

3. Use your eyes to connect both your right and left brain by looking up, to the right, down and to the left.

4. Then repeat this simple phrase that introduces new possibility of thought to your other-than-conscious mind: "I wonder how long before I think or feel something different."

Creating a personal "Stop Button" to release old automatic beliefs is the final step in raising consciousness and an important prerequisite for building new positive thoughts that can enhance self-esteem and build confidence.

AFFIRMATIONS

The second part of *Coaching to the Core* involves the creation of **affirmations** or new positive messages to give to ourselves every day. We need internal statements that reinforce our core being and nourish our basic emotional needs. This process of self-love helps us to feel effective and valued. If we consistently affirm our capacity to be loving and loved by others, I believe that we will feel more valued and secure.

There are many ways to affirm your individuality and uniqueness. Using *affirmations that relate to your basic emotional needs* is very effective for developing a positive sense of self and an improved level of confidence. Below I have listed several affirming statements that you can use as a starting point for your own self-talk. I encourage you to develop your own messages and belief statements that effectively validate your individuality. What is most important in this process is that you choose positive statements that you can embrace and believe. Then you need to dedicate yourself to saying them on a daily basis to reprogram the old internal tapes.

Affirmations strengthen self-image and build confidence.

Remember, this process of *Coaching to the Core*, is just a starting point for building greater self-esteem and confidence. If you begin to consistently give yourself loving compassion, you will be stronger and more empowered to embrace your identity. You will improve your ability to be authentic and more capable of asking others to accept you for who you are. The following are sample affirmations that can strengthen your self-image and build confidence.

Connection
- I love myself
- I am loved by others
- I have fulfilling relationships
- I am a generous and loving person
- I feel special and am a loving partner
- I am an important part of my family

Effectiveness
- I am capable of achieving my dreams
- I am unique with my own special gifts and talents
- I am creative, resourceful and whole
- I am effective and talented in my own way
- I am strong and able to accomplish great things
- I am capable of learning new things

Valued
- I am valued by others for my special gifts and talents
- I am esteemed by others
- I am good person
- I am a good friend to others
- I am generous, loving and kind
- I am a beautiful individual that others want to know

Predictability
- I am confident that life changes are good
- I have the power to change my life
- I flow with change like a river flows with nature
- I learn from life and grow with change
- I accept experiences as lessons for the future
- I have the capacity to change

Security
- I am secure in who I am
- I trust the Universe to take care of me
- I feel nurtured and safe
- I believe in the abundance of opportunity
- I know that the world is full of possibilities
- I always find a way to meet life's challenges and to succeed

Discover Your Potential

To continue the process of discovery, you may want to reflect on the messages that you received in your childhood and journal about how these messages influenced and/or shaped your life.

- What positive messages were the most significant?

- What negative messages still linger with you today?

- In which situations is it easy for you to have confidence and pride in who you are?

- Under what circumstances is it most difficult to feel confident?

- What are some of the ways you nourish your self-esteem?

I WANT

VISION

Helen Keller, the quintessential champion of achievement over adversity, once shared her belief that *we need not pity the person who has no sight, but we should feel sorry for the person who has no vision.* She was a gifted and insightful person with a remarkably astute mind despite her severe disabilities. She became my childhood hero, and the essence of her words still resonates with me today. Helen Keller's life embodied the definition of vision: *Hope for the future.*

Visions are the internal expression of what you want. They are your hope for the future. As part of the process of becoming sentient, you need awareness of what you want to have and what you want to become. Clarity of your vision strengthens your ability to reach your potential. When a vision is magnetic and alluring, you are drawn to it and more motivated to pursue your goals, dreams, and hope for the future. With a clear vision of what you desire, it becomes easier to pull away from that which is undesirable or unfulfilling in your life. A compelling vision energizes your actions and helps you stay on the path toward your potential.

In our childhood, so many of us had an abundance of wonderful visions for our future. Hopes and dreams were like the cotton candy of our mind – sweet and delicious as they swirled through and crystallized in our thoughts. The effervescence of youth held dreams as if they were magical dust that sprinkled itself on our lives. We were only limited by our imagination. Carefree and creative, we energetically pushed forward toward our future.

Somewhere between our youthful innocence and the dogmatic dictates of adult society, it seems that many of us lose the art of dreaming. With the pressures of growing up and facing our adult responsibilities, including the economic and social demands of caring for ourselves, tending to our families, and successfully navigating the world of work,

> **We need not pity the person who has no sight, but we should feel sorry for the person who has no vision.**

it seems that many individuals simply accept the mediocrity of their lives or, worse yet, dwell on their problems. They don't dare to dream.

When asked if they are fulfilled and/or living the life they most desire, many respond with an emphatic "no," but they fail to articulate what it is that would make them happy. They appear to have no hope that things will change because they have no vision. Or even though they still cling to their youthful dreams, they are frustrated because they don't know how to transform dreams into reality. So, they live passively with their status quo.

I contrast these grown-ups with their youthful counterparts and wonder: What happened to the daydreams that fueled their spirit of hope and allowed them to unfailingly persevere toward their goals? What happened to the exuberant child-ish dreams and creative goals that they set without regard for achievability? What burst their bubble of imagination as they traveled the growth highway from child-hood to becoming an adult?

There most certainly is a gap between the irrational childlike enthusiasm for "any-thing is possible" and the rigid confines of adult reality. It appears that this chasm has a lot to do with the messages we hear along the way and the beliefs that are reinforced by individuals such as our parents, peers and professors.

For example, when we were children, our parents nurtured our make-believe and rewarded our imagination with loving approval. When we were young, according to our proud parents, we could "be anything we want" and "do anything we want." We were rarely contradicted with negating comments like "That is not possible."

Limiting beliefs limit vision. Somehow, on the way to becoming self-sufficient adults, many of us experienced a shift in our parents' messages. They changed their attitude about our dreams as their own fears and insecurities crept into their reinforcement of our behavior. These well-meaning adults wanted their children to be secure and to achieve "reasonable" goals. Therefore, many of them discouraged flamboyant dreams with the potential for greatness in favor of "safe" and predictable goals. These parents reinforced a stifling pattern of mediocrity. In many of our families, this pattern has continued from generation to generation.

This pattern mirrors what we learned in the exploration of core beliefs: There appears to be a correlation between the expectations of our parents (together with their inability to dream outside the proverbial box) and the extent to which we, as adults, are able to develop magnificent visions for ourselves. It is very simple to explain: Limiting beliefs limit vision.

But this is not the whole story. Not every adult has lost the ability to visualize and achieve his/her aspirations. Some adults are quite proficient at developing dreams that translate into successful accomplishments. Some of these adults had parental support, and some did not. We all know people who have survived adversity and overcome great odds to achieve extraordinary things despite lack of parental support and/or a nurturing environment.

So what is it that nurtures or inhibits an adult's ability to have and hold a vision? There are several factors that have the potential to strengthen or weaken a person's capacity to pursue grown-up visions including: a nurturing support system, strong self-confidence or a tenacious spirit. But it is difficult to identify which of these is the most influential in developing and/or destroying dreams.

Without a definitive answer, another question comes to mind: *Do all adults have visions?* The answer is, yes, they all have the innate propensity to create visions. As children, it was so easy for them to imagine the future and play make-believe because they knew they had their whole life ahead of them, and visioning was just a part of the process of growing up. They could pretend anything they wanted, and they creatively planned their life with a youthful spirit of innocence that was unencumbered by reality. At some level, adults retain that same childlike inclination to imagine what they desire.

So looking at grown-ups, with their real-life situations already in progress, the next question is *what motivates adults to develop* **new** *visions?* Adults create visions when they are motivated to change. The intensity of that motivation determines whether or not they pursue their adult aspirations.

There are two basic reasons why people develop a new or different vision for themselves. They are *escaping from* something (pain) or they are *attracted to* something (possibility). Some adults may want to escape from a negative situation, and some may want to go for an unfulfilled dream. These two avenues – propulsion from pain and attraction toward desire – are powerful motivators of change. However, both necessitate leaving a current situation and giving up the status quo.

So with an intense motivation, why do some people take action and risk leaving the status quo and others are unable to make this move? The reason is fear. What is this fear all about? Where does it come from? Fear is an expression of insecurity. As we discovered earlier in this book, *insecurity can be experienced whenever an emotional need is not met.*

Change of any kind involves stepping out of our safety zone. For some, even an adverse situation has a sense of structure, because it has some predictability. Moving away from a bad situation involves moving toward the unknown, and this can result in fear. For some this fear is strong enough to inhibit the desire to change. The need to escape the pain or negative situation is overshadowed by the fear that, with change, emotional needs will not be met, and life will be even more unpredictable and less fulfilling.

A vivid portrayal of this phenomenon is the example of a woman living in a situation of domestic abuse. The woman desires a better life for herself and her children – she dreams of being free of the daily abuse and pain. However, fear of failure pierces her dream, and insecurity sets in: "I can't do this," "I won't be able to make it on my own," "I will never be safe," or "I am not smart enough to survive without him." She ultimately does not risk leaving the safety structure of her status quo and resigns herself to give up her vision. The fear of not knowing if her emotional needs will be fulfilled may be enough to keep her where she is and, denying logic, hoping that "everything will be okay."

There are other individuals for whom life is not adverse, but they still have a dream for making their life better. These people want to change the status quo and are motivated to move toward a vision. However, for some, fear ultimately impedes their ability to take action. Again, it is the fear that their emotional needs will not be met that inhibits or destroys the desire to change. They give up their vision and decide to accept the familiar safety structure of their status quo.

We all know the man who is in the "just OK" corporate job that doesn't ignite his passion but pays well and provides for the economic needs of his family. While he desires more creativity, flexibility, and autonomy from his career, he resigns himself to stay where he is because of the fear that he won't be able to get another job or succeed on his own. Once again, the vision is denied in favor of the comfort of the safety structure of the status quo.

These are examples of individuals who, when faced with the opportunity to change to something better, let their insecurities stop them. They focus on their fear which produces limiting beliefs that ultimately keep them from pursuing their dream. Since we all experience insecurity at different times in our life, especially when attempting something new, the question remains: *Why is it that some individuals are still able to pursue and achieve a desired dream in spite of feelings of fear?*

MATURE VISION PARADIGM
To answer this question, here is a paradigm that explains why some people are successful in bringing their adult dreams to fruition and others are not. The secret

lies in the individual's ability to create a ***mature*** vision – a vision that can withstand the pragmatic or negative pressures of reality. A mature vision evolves from **realistic** imagination because it is created in conjunction with a *new* well-defined structure that keeps the individual focused on his goal. With a mature vision and a new safety structure, energy can be focused on the positive, not on the painful or negative situation, and the individual can stay motivated to progress toward his or her dream.

In essence, adults must evolve from the **creative imagination** of childhood dreams and learn to develop the **realistic imagination** of adult aspirations. This allows us to understand why some adults ***surrender*** their vision and others are able to ***champion*** their vision.

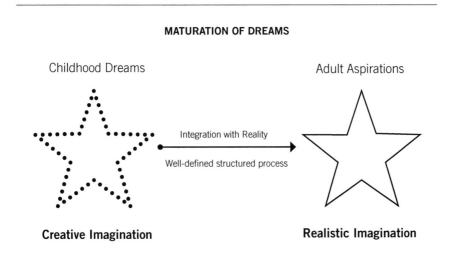

MATURATION OF DREAMS

Childhood Dreams　　　　　　　　　　Adult Aspirations

Integration with Reality

Well-defined structured process

Creative Imagination　　　　　　**Realistic Imagination**

There is a continuum between youthful exuberance and adult aspirations. The movement away from the creative imagination of childhood involves continuous integration with reality. As we develop and mature, our visions need to mature with us to withstand the insecurities and fear inherent in trying to change our reality. In theory, every individual has the same opportunity to move along this continuum and successfully develop and achieve adult dreams. But only those individuals who have the clarity and magnetic power of a mature vision, *together with* a well-defined action plan (structured process) to keep fear at a minimum, will be able to stay focused and motivated to make their vision happen.

What happens for many people is there is a point on their growth journey at which they meet a form of **reality resistance**, and their ability to create a new vision is diminished or lost. These individuals suffer a loss of hope, adopt an "I can't do this" mentality, and ultimately slip into the comfortable conformity of accepting the status quo. When faced with the practical pressures and restricted thinking of others, they "cop out" and surrender their visions.

By contrast, there are others who appear to have exceptional tenacity and a willingness to persevere in the face of resistance. These individuals not only allow their dreams to mature, but they also adapt their approach and use their maturity to develop a form of **realistic imagination** coupled with a well-defined structured process that keeps fear and insecurity to a minimum and ultimately enables them to stay motivated and focused on their vision. These are the people who are most likely to bring their adult aspirations to fruition.

Their vision is so magnetic and clear that they strive to do whatever is necessary to achieve their goal. An alluring vision coupled with a structured approach to "make it happen" is what brings success. The more magnetic the vision, the more likely that individuals will be pulled toward achieving it, and the more willing they will be to let go of the resistance to obstacles in their way. Individuals who use realistic visions to stay focused on their goals increase the potential for achieving their dream. For some, the vision may be crystal clear and well-defined. They can visualize it vividly in their mind and articulate the specific details of their dream. Others don't have that clarity or specificity at first, but they do have what I call "visceral vision" that serves the same purpose.

A visceral vision is just as powerful as a clear and well-defined vision in that it has a magnetic power that evokes passion and energy. With a visceral vision, when the individual thinks about what it would *feel* like to achieve a dream, he or she experiences positive energy that infuses the soul as if the dream were really alive. In a sense, the person feels as if all emotional needs are being met. These emotions are *felt every day* as the individual journeys toward the end goal. The daily energy and emotional feelings feed the motivation to stay on course.

Whether it is a vivid or visceral vision, individuals can experience the magnetic power of attraction toward their goal, without the complete knowledge of *how* to make it happen. As long as there is a structured approach to provide daily discipline to complement their emotional commitment, individuals can stay focused on their dream. They hold firm to the positive *impulse* of their vision and let the *form* stay flexible. As they progress, the structured approach will provide the framework that ultimately defines the fine details of their dream and the *how* to make it happen. Later in this chapter, we will describe the process through which one can move from a visceral vision to a vivid vision that has more clarity and definition.

Those who are successful with the process of using realistic imagination to create mature visions rely on *metaphysics* and the *power of creative thinking* in concert with their personal conviction and dedication. On a daily basis they affirm their dream as if it were reality. In doing so, they focus their energy to move tenaciously toward their goal in spite of any lingering doubts and habitual insecurities. The most triumphant ones earnestly follow the advice of American author Napoleon Hill, who once said, "Cherish your visions and your dreams as they are the children of your soul."

We have all seen illustrations of this paradigm in the achievements of celebrities and great leaders. Martin Luther King had a vision to which he was faithfully committed. Indeed, his most famous and eloquent sermon delivered on the steps of the Lincoln Memorial in Washington, D.C. in 1963 was

> **"Cherish your visions and your dreams as they are the children of your soul."**
> – Napoleon Hill

titled "I have a dream." Robert F. Kennedy is remembered for his famous words: "Some men see things as they are and ask 'Why'. I dream of things that never were, and ask 'Why not?'" And Christopher Reeve, our famous Superman, who struggled to overcome his insurmountable physical challenges until the day he died, once said, "So many of our dreams at first seem impossible, then they seem improbable, and then, when we summon the will, they soon become inevitable."

One of the best portrayals of *how* to use the power of creative thought with a structured action plan to achieve success was demonstrated by one of the greatest Olympic champions of all time, swimmer John Naber, who in 1976 won four gold medals and one silver, setting four world records and becoming the first Olympic swimmer in history to win two individual medals on the same day.

In the book he compiled and edited, *Awaken the Olympian Within*, John Naber shares his belief that "our willingness to invest in our dreams is inevitably related to our confidence that the dreams are actually attainable. It's hard to bet confidently on a long shot, but once we feel the possibility of success, the work involved is more easily produced." When I met John Naber several years ago, he passionately explained to me how he did just that – set an ambitious specific goal and then tenaciously affirmed the *feelings* of success on a daily basis for four years – to achieve the phenomenal victory that he did. Here is his story:

John was a senior in high school watching an Olympic swimming world record holder win the race he, John himself, swam competitively. Extremely bright and creative, John extrapolated the champion's winning times from the 1968 and 1972 Olympics to determine what the winning time would most likely be four years hence. The time, 55.5 seconds was a tremendous stretch for John, whose lowest time was 59.5 or four (huge!) seconds more. But that didn't matter to a young man who committed himself to that vision of winning the 1976 Olympics in a time that had never been done before.

And so began his journey with a decisive goal upon which to focus. He wrote that ambitious time goal on a piece of paper which he then taped to his bathroom mirror to look at every morning and night. Creating a **vision** was the first step toward what John calls Gold Medal Performance© – the **structure** by which he lived for four years in pursuit of his dream. John's structure included his commitment and dedication to planning and hard work. He developed measurable goals to create his rigorous training schedule. And he continuously pushed himself forward to implement his plan despite obstacles and the pressures of performance.

Without question, John admitted to me, the most important factor that contributed to his success was the daily visualization that he used to affirm his dream. Each and every night, right before he went to sleep, John used his power of creative thought and realistic imagination *to see and feel* his success **in his mind**. He felt the energy of sweeping through the water at the Olympics as he heard the roaring applause and shouts from the exuberant spectators watching his event. He imagined and felt the magnificence of passing by the previous Olympian as he pushed himself to victory. Every day for four years, in his mind, John Naber triumphantly won his Olympic swimming event with the record-breaking time that was taped to his mirror.

On the day that he actually swam for the United States in the finals of the 1976 Olympics, John Naber set a world record with his Gold Medal winning time of 55.49 seconds. His victory was just 1/100th of a second off the optimistic goal he had set four years earlier and taped to his bathroom mirror. Not only did he make history, but John demonstrated for all of us how the power of vision together with focused energy, hard work and dedication can make dreams come true.

John Naber's secret to success is actually available to all of us even though we may not be Olympic champions or competitive athletes. We all have the ability to create powerful visions and bring them to fruition. Furthermore, there is an abundance of information available to us, about metaphysics and the laws of energy that shows us how to create the well-defined structure necessary to make our dreams reality. Some of these are listed in the **Links to Potential** section at the end of this chapter if you are interested in reading and learning more about this subject.

The model presented here is derived from the basic principles in the science of metaphysics, the branch of philosophy that examines the nature of reality and the relationship between the mind and physical matter. The heart of metaphysics is the theory that what we think and believe will manifest itself in our life. This cognitive science and philosophy of mind celebrates the creative ability of our consciousness. Metaphysics is closely tied to the practice of manifestation, or the act of bringing something into existence and reality.

With the practice of metaphysics, there is a presumption that in order to direct your life circumstances, not only do you need to create new thoughts, but you must first release old thoughts that contradict or interfere with your new desires. The process of letting go of old beliefs is one that was explored in an earlier chapter where you evaluated ingrained beliefs that either support or limit your potential. These same internalized messages can affect the quality of your visions and your ability to manifest them as reality. As we discovered, positive beliefs reinforce your self-image and support your emotional growth while negative, or limiting, beliefs limit your ability to achieve goals and your capacity to thrive.

Manifestation, or the power to transform your visions into reality, is inextricably linked to your awareness of self. You need to be able to use your awareness (self-knowledge), together with the power of focused energy, to intentionally create that which you most desire. It is very simple. To reach your highest vision, you need to have awareness of two things: *What you want* and *how to get it!* These two concepts – **Discovery and Development** – are complementary and essential elements of the manifestation process.

Discovery is the awareness and articulation of your desired vision, which then must be coupled with the Development of a structure that can support your vision and withstand the pressures of reality. In combination, you can focus your energy, affirm and visualize your goal, and dedicate yourself to the process of manifesting your reality.

Discovery involves not only generating a clear and articulate vision of what you want but, more importantly, creating a powerful magnetic vision that produces a "visceral energy." This kind of vision has the lasting power to consistently motivate you toward your goal. A visceral vision brings you to the exciting edge of possibility. When a vision becomes visceral, it is *felt* with every fiber of your being. You don't just think it – you own it, and then it becomes intertwined with your mind, body and spirit.

Development will be unique for each of us. We all have different needs as to the type of structure, regimen or process we need to stay energized and focused on pursuing our vision. John Naber's structured training and action plan, to which he committed himself on a daily basis for four years, is an excellent example of a well-developed structure that provided safety and continuous nourishment of a vision until it was delivered.

Discovery and Development are like fraternal twins, traveling hand-in-hand on a metaphysical journey. Like siblings, they support each other – the awareness (self-knowledge) and action (development) components of vision and manifestation. These components must always coexist.

> **Awareness without action renders the knowledge useless.**
> **Action without awareness results in futile dreams.**

DIAMOND DREAMS

Our dreams, not unlike ourselves, are akin to diamonds – beautiful, precious and valuable gems. Each dream is unique and multifaceted. We treasure our dreams and adult aspirations just as we treasure diamonds Dreams and diamonds…the analogy is very powerful and strong.

Diamonds were formed deep in the Earth billions of years ago. A diamond is made of carbon in its most concentrated form, and it exists deep within the earth for long periods of time under conditions of tremendous heat and pressure. It is this intense pressure and heat that ultimately turns the carbon into crystalline or diamond as we know it. Because they form at such great depths, diamonds only ascend to the Earth's surface through the mighty force of an erupting volcano. And even then, they remain extremely rare, and it takes sophistication to mine them.

A nearly pure, brilliant crystalline of carbon, the diamond is the hardest of all gemstones known to man, yet it is the simplest in composition. The hardness, brilliance and sparkle of diamonds make them unsurpassed as precious gems.

The word diamond can be traced to the Greek word "Adamas" which means invincible or unconquerable. Ancient Greeks believed that diamonds were splinters of stars that had fallen to earth. Over time diamonds became associated with strength, invulnerability and magical qualities. In today's culture, diamonds symbolize wealth, brilliance and unsurpassed quality. A diamond is the magnificent monarch of gems. It remains supreme with its capacity to glitter, dazzle, and symbolize love, beauty and strength.

Diamonds have imperfections, and yet they radiate and shine! Every one is different, and each is treasured for its composite qualities. Diamonds, just like our dreams, don't stand alone. They have settings, or structures, that hold them firmly in place. The setting forms the safety structure that supports the diamond's beauty and allows us to cherish it even more.

Just like mining for diamonds, you need to dig deep to discover your visions and yourself. Oftentimes, at first glance, a vision may seem rough or undefined. If it lacks clarity it needs to be polished. Polishing is a fine art that ultimately illuminates the inner brilliance. Remember that diamonds gain their strength under pressure, and it takes many years in transformation to yield the treasured gem.

DIGGING FOR DIAMONDS: *Discover Your Vision*

Ask yourself: What dreams do you have for your future? What do you want? Where would you like to be? What would you like to become?

Let the vision be just like a rough diamond. With time, you will be able to refine and polish the image to add greater clarity.

- What would it feel like to experience and have your dream come true?

- Don't worry about the "how to make it happen," just stay in a place of "being" with your dream.

- Dream BIG! Discovery is all about dreams and desire.

- Contrast what you have to what you want: If you would like more clarity, look at what you *don't want*, and turn each thought around into a *do want*. If necessary, take a piece of paper and draw a line down the middle. On the left column write a thought that represents what you *don't want*, and then immediately, on the other side of the page, contrast that thought with a *do want*. Once you have formulated your positive desire, cross out the negative don't-want message. Continue the process with as many thoughts as you need to express your desires in relation to a particular part of your life.

- If possible, think of your "wishes and wants" in words or a visual image. Perhaps you will only have a visceral feeling of excitement or joy as you think about what it would feel like to achieve your goals. Hold on to this feeling – this is the "visceral vision." This can bring you to the exciting edge of possibility.

- Remember, it takes years and a lot of heat and pressure to turn carbon into a diamond. It may take a long time for you to get *crystal clarity* with your image. You may have to cut and reshape your initial idea to get the best gem.

- The vision doesn't have to be a *reality*. Just affirm the *possibility* in your heart.

- Hold firm to the initial impulse, and let the final form unfold naturally.

Say Something Simple!

- As you hold your image, with all its desirable possibilities in your heart, think about what is really most valuable: YOU.

- Each day treasure your identity, your gifts and desires as the real gems.

- Every day **Say Something Simple** (your daily affirmation) to positively affirm your internal spirit and energize the vision of what you want in your life.

This same process was used by an experienced saleswoman named Tina, who had twenty years of experience selling a variety of different products and services. She had reached the pinnacle of her career right before the turn of the millennium, earning in excess of $100,000 per year. She had a natural salesperson's mentality and was extremely organized, persistent and tenacious. Like so many other seasoned professionals, post 9/11 in the year 2001, she was laid off from a company that was not doing well. After several months of unemployment, she was finally able to secure a "commission only" position working for a very small advertising company.

When Tina started her new position, she was enthusiastic and confident that she would not only enjoy the creative sales process but, with her many years of experience, would surely meet the revenue goals and expectations of her new boss. To help cover expenses during the early months of her tenure with the company, Tina received a modest "draw against commission." Right from the start, she owed the company money, but that did not dilute her enthusiasm or deter her from methodically working her territory as she had always done. In her mind, if she would just follow her proven pattern of calling, setting appointments and building relationships with prospective clients, she would meet her goals.

Within a few months of employment, it became clear that her boss' style of management was very different from the leadership approach that had allowed Tina to be most effective in the past. The owner of the company (her boss) was demanding, confrontational, and unrelenting in her expectations. Tina began to feel the negative effects of the environment in which she worked. Her sales suffered, and so did her health. She did not feel effective, valued, or at all engaged with her boss and the company. Her debt mounted, and her health declined.

When Tina first learned about this process for developing her dream, she was resistant. Instead she focused on the pathology of the situation and remained disgusted with her boss, frustrated with her increasing debt, and hopeless that things would change. She poured her mental energy into these negative thoughts, and so, nothing changed. Eventually, her closest friends wrapped their arms around her – literally and figuratively. They persuaded her that she had nothing to lose by dreaming her dream. On the contrary, by *hoping and believing* that "the impossible" would come true – that she could work her way out of debt, leave the company and find another *better* position – her vision just might become her reality.

Tina's friends gave her the affirmations that acknowledged her competence and asked her to say them every day to affirm her worth. They encouraged her to close her eyes, picture in her mind what it would look like to be free (from the job, the overbearing boss, and her debt), and they insisted that she keep believing in the power of the Universe to provide a solution to her situation.

With nothing to lose and everything to gain, Tina embraced their ideas and began to repeat her affirmations, visualize new opportunities, and transform her energy on a daily basis. Within a month her confidence returned, and she decided to leave the company to preserve her health, even though she still had $10,000 of debt owed to her boss. She gave her two weeks of notice and continued to hope for the best. She visualized her dream of getting what she wanted while she methodically made her sales calls each day.

On the day before she was planning to leave the company, her phone rang and suddenly her dreams of *possibility* became her reality! The man on the other end of the phone was a buyer for a major manufacturer. He needed a huge splashy advertising campaign to announce a revolutionary new product in the digital entertainment industry. Tina held her breath and calmly handled the call. Before she hung up, she had sold him $20,000 worth of advertising – erasing her debt and buying her freedom! She and her friends celebrated that night with a triumphant toast: "If you can dream it, you can achieve it!" Tina had.

DEVELOP THE SETTING FOR YOUR DIAMOND DREAMS

Tina's glittering dreams may be similar to yours. But just as precious stones need a setting to hold them secure, you will need to develop a structure that supports your vision. The development of a structure ensures that you stay focused and motivated to achieve your goal. Just like the diamond's setting, the framework will support your vision and help it to radiate and shine. Creating the energy and committing to action are the guideposts of your setting. They form the foundation for the structure that holds your dreams steady and firm.

The process of refining and polishing your diamond dreams creates energy. When you create a framework for pursuing your goals, you can focus that energy. You need energy to intellectually and physically achieve your goals. When you hold firm to the *feelings* associated with your dreams, you generate new energy or vibrations of possibility. This new energy in turn attracts opportunities to you. This attraction is a powerful force in manifesting reality.

COMMIT TO ACTION

The development of an action plan will be unique to each of us. We all have different needs as to the type of structure, regime or process we need to stay energized and focused on our vision. The structure can be an elaborate business plan, a simple to do list, or a series of mini-goals that serve as stepping stones on the journey. We will explore "Action Plans" in greater detail in a later chapter. For now, these are a few thoughts that may be helpful as you prepare to commit to action:

- Choose whatever structure works best for you to develop purposeful actions that will keep you motivated and energized every day. Some people define this as "Discipline." The act of developing a plan, to which you are committed every day, can also be seen as "Acting with Purpose."

- *Acting with Purpose* is part of the diamond refining process. With each step of the journey, you may cut, refine and add clarity to your vision.

- Each new phase will have its own brilliance and sense of possibility.

- As you work your plan, you will naturally create new energy that revitalizes and reinforces your spirit and your dreams.

These definitive steps for developing the setting that holds your vision secure are designed to support your process of growth. The setting for your dreams is just another way to keep you focused and energized, but – more than that – it is a methodology for building and maintaining confidence as you pursue your treasured visions.

Diamond dreams...they are rare, unique, valuable and treasured gems of our lives. We all have the ability to dream, as well as the ability to manifest those dreams as reality. When you stay committed and passionately focused on your diamond dreams – allowing those dreams to be polished, re-cut and refined as life necessitates, you open yourself up to greater possibility. Ultimately, you can confidently create a treasure chest of opportunity for fulfillment in your life.

DISCOVER YOUR POTENTIAL

To continue the process of discovery, you may want to reflect on:

- What were the childhood dreams that energized my spirit?

- What are the goals that I have thought about but not pursued as an adult?

- What do I want most in my life that I don't have now?

- Where would I like to be in five years? What would I be doing? Where would I be living? How would my life be different from what it is today?

- What would it look like to be living my highest vision?

LINKS TO POTENTIAL

Special thanks to John Naber for his story from his book *Awaken the Olympian Within*. www.JohnNaber.com

Some of the more well-known authors on the subject of harnessing the energy to get what you want are listed below. All of these authors, although different in style, offer practical guides to manifesting your dreams. They each have unique advice for developing your intuition, working with the power of intentionality, and harnessing the energy to get what you most want in your life.

- *The Seven Spiritual Laws of Success: A Practical Guide to the Fulfillment of Your Dreams* by Deepak Chopra

- *The Circle* and *Practical Intuition* by Laura Day

- *Manifest Your Destiny* and *The Power of Intention* by Dr. Wayne Dyer

- *The Power is Within You* and Power Thought Cards by Louise Hay

- *Unlimited Power* by Tony Robbins

- Gail Straub and David Gershon, founders of the internationally recognized Empowerment Institute, have become leading authorities on manifestation and personal transformation. Since 1981, when they first introduced their highly acclaimed empowerment workshop, they have trained thousands of individuals throughout the world. You may enjoy reading their book *Empowerment: The Art of Creating Your Life as You Want It* or visiting their Website at: www.EmpowermentTraining.com.

I WILL

ACTION

Action is an interesting word with numerous implications. The thesaurus suggests words like *Achievement* and *Accomplishment* as synonyms for Action. The dictionary defines "act" with words like *do something, take steps,* and *proceed* or *move toward.* When we look at the other two descriptive meanings of action, *achievement* and *accomplishment,* there is a more definitive sense of completion to the word as opposed to the idea of *initiating* something, which is what we do when we start to act.

So what does *action* really mean for you? As you continue on your journey of discovery, does it mean to *do something, to take steps* and *proceed?* Or does Action mean *achievement* and *accomplishment?* It means all of the above. In fact, these synonyms perfectly describe what you need to do to reach your goal.

Earlier in this book, we defined Action as the external expression of what we want or the process of making our visions a reality. We began our process of discovery with self-awareness of our identity and an understanding of what it means to be authentic. Then we went digging for diamonds to uncover our precious visions and treasured dreams. And now it is time to proceed toward our vision and turn our dreams into reality with purposeful action.

In this context, action is not random activity. It is purposeful, deliberate progress. You have created your visions, and you can create your life. You know who you are, you know what you want, and now it is time to be. You have the power to *be*, and with that comes the power to *do* – to do something, to take action, and to create the life you envision.

As you have done throughout your journey, you must look inside and then look ahead. Everything you need to be successful and fulfilled is inside of you. With knowledge of self, you own your strength and your power. And that forceful energy is what will propel you toward your vision.

Your path to power begins with one step, and as you proceed on your journey you will define your plan and make progress toward your goal. You cannot get to your vision without action. Additionally, if you live in the present moment, taking action one day at a time, you can **be** who you are – trusting your truth, *and* trusting that the Universe will provide the outcomes you need if you stay committed to your vision, your actions and yourself.

To walk your path you need courage. Courage comes from *being* who you are, trusting your truth (intuition), and living each day the best that you can. A simple reminder: "The only courage that matters is the kind that gets you from one moment to the next." (Mingnon McLaughlin)

Your visions form the endpost of your journey, but the path itself is also important. Your visions are like stars in the sky. You can reach for your stars with hope, faith and confidence as you take action. Achievements and accomplishments are the rewards for taking action. To reference Napoleon Hill once again, he connects our dreams to actions with the following quote: "Cherish your visions and your dreams as they are the children of your soul: the blueprints of your ultimate achievements."

> **"The only courage that matters is the kind that gets you from one moment to the next."**
> – Mingnon McLaughlin

Knowing your truth and being authentic frees you to live life passionately and from a place of power. When you are free, you don't have to live life sheltered and protected, nor do you have to pretend to be something you are not. Instead, you are free to use your energy to take action and passionately follow your dreams.

By embracing your values, gifts and vision you have the power to choose actions that support being authentic and consistent with your truth. You must then live your truth every day through your actions.

FROM AUTHENTICITY TO ACTION

With this book, you have embarked on a journey of discovery and an exploration of your potential. In the process, you have come to understand who you are (I AM) with an appreciation for your innate gifts, unique talents and genetic characteristics, as well as your personal strengths. In the next section (I NEED), you discovered what you need to be emotionally fulfilled and authentic and how to have courage and confidence to pursue your promise of potential. In Vision (I WANT), you discovered the nature of your dreams and learned how to dig deep for the precious gems that ignite your passion and hopes for the future.

And finally, this last section is all about your commitment to action. Action (I WILL) is where the rubber meets the road. You know who you are, you know what you want, and now you must act accordingly. You need to live each day aligned with your values as you progress toward your vision. Your actions, even in the face of challenges and adversity, must be authentic and consistent with your true self. It takes commitment and dedication to pursue and achieve your potential.

The following table summarizes the foundational messages of the four sections of this book. As you gain awareness of your identity and vision, you can move from authenticity to action. When you embrace the full knowledge of who you are, you become empowered to develop your full potential.

Identity **I AM**	Authenticity **I NEED**	Vision **I WANT**	Action **I WILL**
Discover Your Truth Trust Your Truth	Declare What You NEED Speak Your Truth	Know What You WANT Create Your Vision	Commit Action Live Your Truth

To move from authenticity to action, you need to understand that your emotions and personal beliefs are not only embedded in your being, but they form the nucleus of your behavior. Emotions and beliefs influence your actions. Some of your beliefs serve you well; others limit your potential and inhibit your growth. When you become entangled in your emotions, you may derail from your course of action or fall from a position of strength and confidence. To take action, let's begin with your emotions.

THE EMOTIONAL LINK TO ACTION

When you experience an emotion, you can trace the feelings back to your basic emotional needs, which are: *the need to feel connected, valued, effective, secure, and able to handle change.* Understanding the relationship between feelings and emotional needs involves self-awareness and assessment of your core beliefs.

The core beliefs we possess are deeply ingrained in our adult being. Originating from a variety of sources, both overt and subtle, a core belief may impact our ability to live as an empowered being *if* the belief does not affirm our self-worth. When a core belief does not serve us well, or interferes with our confidence or the ability to take positive actions, it is defined as a negative or limiting belief. A *limiting belief* does just that: It *limits* our power and inhibits our actions, oftentimes resulting in undesirable emotional thought patterns or destructive behaviors.

If you have a desire to change your behavior, you must first understand the emotions associated with that behavior. Then you must identify the underlying or limiting belief linked to those emotions. Ultimately you need to proactively create a new belief that affirms your self-worth, one that will support positive action in the future. Simply stated, the process of understanding how emotional beliefs relate to actions involves the following steps:

- Identifying the facts of the situation
- Assessing:
    - The emotions triggered by the situation
    - The underlying emotional needs correlated with these feelings
- Evaluating the beliefs that are associated with these emotion – especially the beliefs that do not serve you (limiting beliefs)
- "Turning around" the limiting belief by crafting a positive statement that affirms your self-worth

Transforming a limiting belief into an affirmation sometimes takes a bit of practice. However, because this exercise can empower you to live the life you want, it is worth the effort.

A limiting belief usually appears as an "I should" statement such as "I should be able to control this situation" or "I should know how to handle this." But oftentimes it goes deeper, and the limiting belief shows up as a statement that denounces self-worth: "I am not good enough," "I can't do this" or "I am not smart enough or capable enough."

When our core beliefs derail the confidence we need to act, we must look deeper into our identity and search for something positive that we **can** believe. We will then be able to craft a statement that acknowledges qualities that affirm our being. This "turn-around" statement becomes an **affirmation** that reinforces our innate gifts and unique qualities. "I am capable." "I have the ability to succeed." "I have done this before and successfully achieved my goals in the past." Writing down affirmations makes them more visible and concrete. As you learned with *Coaching to the Core*, repeating an affirmation daily will also help reinforce your emotional needs and build self-confidence.

PREPARING FOR EMPOWERMENT: *Assess / Affirm / Act*
This simple framework will help you understand the emotions and beliefs that interfere with your inner sense of calm in times of emotional stress. You can use this exercise as a mechanism through which you can *assess* your emotions and beliefs, *affirm* your self-worth, and *act* in alignment with your highest poten-

tial. For example, the following describes a situation of a client of mine who is a successful management executive and well-organized professional.

> *Although Monique takes a proactive approach to time management by carefully planning her daily activities, she encounters days when there are unexpected interruptions and demands on her time. Urgent requests, unannounced visitors, and phone calls – all requiring decisive action – put a strain on her personal sense of calm. While she always performs well in the face of disarray, she wants to learn better ways to handle stressful situations. In her mind, she outwardly appears self-possessed but inwardly, she feels anxious and not fully in control of her emotions.*

The following exercise was *empowering* because it allowed her to understand the correlation between her emotional needs and her negative limiting beliefs. Her "turn-around" statement and positive affirmation strengthened her ability to make better decisions. This helped preserve her self-esteem and allowed her to act more confidently. Her turn-around statement was followed by a **purposeful symbolic action** that helped reinforce and practice her new belief.

SAMPLE EMPOWERMENT EXERCISE: *Chaos and challenges at work*

FACT	Chaos at work, circumstances changing rapidly.
EMOTION	I feel frustrated and afraid.
EMOTIONAL NEED	Effectiveness, control and predictability.
LIMITING BELIEF	I am not good enough, or I am afraid of failure. I should be able to control circumstances, or I should be able to predict ebb and flow of work. I am not good enough to fix this chaos effectively.
TURN-AROUND	I am organized. I am courageous. I am calm and capable of assessing situations and prioritizing what I need to do.
PURPOSEFUL SYMBOLIC ACTION	Each morning I will prioritize my list of activities and schedule one hour of time (do not disturb) to accomplish my tasks.

In this example, chaos and rapid change led to unexpected emotions of inadequacy. The individual may have had a distorted sense of her ability to cope. Her self-image was further compromised when she felt a need to control and an expectation that she should be able to control circumstances. While control was the essential issue, the sense of frustration came from allocating the expectation of control to the wrong thing. As in my client's case, this phenomenon is more likely to occur with an individual who prefers order and a structured daily routine.

You, no doubt, understand that an individual who thrives on discipline, pre-planning, and an organized time-management process is more likely to feel a loss of control when external circumstances interrupt or diminish the well-structured sense of order. When the individual's need for order and predictability are disrupted by external circumstances, negative emotions such as feeling frustrated, out of control and ineffective may result.

For some people, it may be an overpowering fear of failure that blocks their ability to problem solve and effectively navigate through chaos. These negative emotions, while generated from external circumstances, are directly tied to personal core beliefs. Understanding the powerful correlation between the emotions and beliefs that inhibit our ability to act is, therefore, critically important to developing good problem-solving skills and achieving life success.

As presented, this empowerment exercise allows an individual to better understand emotional responses by exploring underlying limiting beliefs and turning them into positive statements. Once an affirmation is declared and a new behavior or purposeful symbolic action is defined, the individual can begin to develop new emotional responses or emotional *habits* that better serve them.

A purposeful symbolic action serves as the catalyst for ultimately changing behavior. Using the model described above, many clients were able to evaluate a variety of circumstances that involved negative feelings triggered from unfulfilled emotional needs. In each situation, the clients were asked to identify the ingrained beliefs associated with their emotions and to assess how these limited their ability to act.

They developed **"turn-around"** statements from each **limiting belief** and created positive affirmations to restore a positive sense of self. With consistent practice, they acquired new ways to handle stressful situations and became more empowered and motivated to act in harmony with their potential.

In stressful or challenging situations, the **turn-around process** described above is only a first step toward self-empowerment. **Once an individual articulates an affirmation that is self-reinforcing, he or she can methodically move from authenticity to action by acknowledging what he or she needs, wants, and is**

willing to do to achieve personal goals. The purposeful symbolic action described above is the first step toward self-empowerment, action planning and personal transformation.

DISCOVERING YOUR COMMITMENT TO ACTION

The transformation of a limiting belief into a commitment to action can be expressed by four simple phrases:

I AM / I NEED / I WANT / I WILL

These phrases form the framework for empowering self-talk or engaging in conversations that support action. These words are easy to remember and can help you move forward from emotional stagnation caused by limiting beliefs. This process reaffirms the strengths of your **identity** together with the magnetism of your **vision** and allows you to generate a definitive commitment to **action**. Here is how this self-empowerment and action planning technique works:

- Your "Turn-around" statement correlates with your IDENTITY.
- From that position, you can assess what you NEED.
- With self-awareness for your truth (Identity) and your needs (Authenticity), you can create a VISION for what you want.
- Then you can commit to what you will do (ACTION) to achieve your vision.

Identity **I AM**	Authenticity **I NEED**	Vision **I WANT**	Action **I WILL**

The steps of this model use the simple phrases: I AM / I NEED / I WANT / I WILL. The sequence begins with affirming your identity and discovering your own truth. With true authenticity, you can declare what you need by speaking your truth. When you are authentic, you can express what you want and reaffirm your vision. As an outgrowth of this natural progression, you will be aligned with your truth and able to commit to action.

Identity **I AM**	Authenticity **I NEED**	Vision **I WANT**	Action **I WILL**
Discover Your Truth Trust Your Truth	Declare What You NEED Speak Your Truth	Know What You WANT Create Your Vision	Commit Action Live Your Truth

Let's take a look at how this model can be used to explore commitment to personal goals. The following is an empowerment exercise that a client used recently to explore her desire to become a certified aerobics instructor teaching workout classes.

SAMPLE EMPOWERMENT EXERCISE: *Personal Goals/Professional Career*

FACT	I promised myself I would be an aerobics instructor.
EMOTION	I feel scared, challenged, and afraid of failure.
EMOTIONAL NEED	Need to feel effective.
LIMITING BELIEF	I am not good enough to be certified for training. I can't commit to a long-term plan. I won't be able to get a job as an instructor.
TURN-AROUND	I have strong motivation, energy and physical capabilities. I always succeed when I love what I do. I feel better when I exercise and commit to a regular routine. I have been an instructor in the past.
PURPOSEFUL SYMBOLIC ACTION	Each morning I will prioritize my list of activities and schedule one hour of time (do not disturb) to accomplish my tasks.

She began by restating her goal. She then identified her feelings and assessed the beliefs that limited her ability to move toward her goal. Finally, by crafting a turn-around statement from her limiting belief, she was able to focus on the positive energy that would ultimately help her move forward.

This exercise was a critical first step of committing to action. The foundational work of understanding her emotions and limiting beliefs allowed her to assess what she needed to do to achieve her dreams. Empowering self-talk created the affirmations that would help commit her goals to action.

EMPOWERMENT ACTION PLAN

The next step was to create an empowerment action plan as shown below:

EMPOWERMENT ACTION PLAN

Identity **I AM**	Authenticity **I NEED**	Vision **I WANT**	Action **I WILL**
Discover "Who I AM" Trust Your Truth	Declare What You NEED Speak Your Truth	Know What You WANT Create Your Vision	Commit to Action Be Willing to Live Your Truth
I am physically fit, and I love exercise. I am good at aerobics, and I have taught classes before. I feel so energized when I teach classes and connect with other people. I always achieve my goals.	I need to set a plan to follow. I need to get back into the routine of classes. I need to apply for certification exam. I need to schedule the certification exam. I need to apply for jobs and plan where/when I would be teaching.	I want my plan written and goals set so that I can be motivated to action. I want to be certified in six months and teaching three classes a week within one year.	I will commit to drafting my plan by the first of next month. By the end of next month I will be working out three times a week and have registered for the classes. In three months I will update my resumé and network. I will take the test within six months.

On the following page is a template that you can use for your own empowerment action planning (you may prefer to transfer this grid to a notebook for more space). This worksheet can help you sort out your emotions and enable you to better understand the beliefs that may be limiting your potential. Use this model whenever you need to assess how you are feeling as it relates to what you are doing, or not doing, in pursuit of your goals.

EMPOWERMENT ACTION PLANNING

Identity **I AM**	Authenticity **I NEED**	Vision **I WANT**	Action **I WILL**
Discover Your Truth Trust Your Truth	Declare What You NEED Speak Your Truth	Know What You WANT Create Your Vision	Commit to Action Be Willing to Align Your Truth
Create affirmations that reinforce who you are:	Create affirmations that declare what you need to be authentic:	Create affirmations that state your vision and the highest ideal for what you want in your life:	

DISCOVER YOUR POTENTIAL

Questions for reflection:

- What are some of the meaningful goals that I have envisioned but not pursued?

- What are some of my fears that have prevented me from taking a course of action?

- What are some of the deep (perhaps unconscious) limiting beliefs that may be related to these fears?

- With which dreams or goals in my personal and professional life might this empowerment exercise be helpful?

- How could I use this exercise to improve my commitment to action with personal and professional relationships?

COMMUNICATION

Communication is the common thread intricately woven in all relationships. It is the process by which ideas are expressed, messages are conveyed, questions are asked, and information is shared. Humans use language and communication to express how they feel, ask for what they need, describe their visions, and declare their commitment to action. The "act of communicating" is prevalent throughout of the process of becoming sentient.

We use communication in all of our relationships. Effective communication is directly linked to building cohesive bonds with family, friends and business associates. Skilled communicators effectively communicate the essence of their ideas, feelings and needs. They also listen deeply, demonstrate empathy and communicate persuasively.

Communication allows us to ask for what we need and want. We have to exchange ideas and negotiate differences in order to commit to a shared vision. Communication is a valuable tool that can help us hold our place of power. It serves us when we need to articulate the strength of our convictions and commitments. From authenticity to action, communication plays a part in helping us reach our potential.

EMPOWERING CONVERSATIONS

In the previous chapter, you learned an exercise that is used by individuals to evaluate how they feel, assess reasons why they may not be working toward a desired goal, and to reaffirm their commitment to action. As we demonstrated, the exercise can be used to initiate "self-talk" if a person is feeling unmotivated, having difficulty taking action, or wants to better understand his or her commitment to personal goals.

This model is easy to apply to a variety of situations both personally and professionally. *Empowering Conversation* is excellent for initiating a conversation with others – a spouse, partner, friend or business colleague. When used with another person, however, it is important to recognize that these empowering conversations are just one part of the communication process.

The exercise employs a great place to start any conversation. It begins with a positive reaffirmation of innate gifts, strengths and positive attributes. It also allows an individual to gain clarity of personal needs and desires before committing to action. To illustrate, here is an example of how one of my clients used this process to understand her feelings and emotional needs in her relationship with her husband.

She talked about how upset she became when she learned that her husband was meeting with female business associates outside of the office. In particular, she didn't like that he was having dinner with another woman. It conjured up all kinds of feelings and pictures in her mind. Using the turn-around process, she explored the emotions and beliefs associated with his having dinner with another woman. She followed the sequence of this model and answered each section with her comments described below.

FACT	My husband is having dinner with another woman.
EMOTION	I feel anger, disappointment, fear and insecurity.
EMOTIONAL NEED	Connection and Value (I am not connected or valued).
LIMITING BELIEF	I should be able to satisfy him totally. I am not enough. I am not loved. I am not enough to satisfy my husband.
TURN-AROUND	I am a loving woman. I am affectionate and caring. I am a good partner, and we both have other friends.

She used the Empowerment Conversation model to assess her feelings, affirm her self worth, and then plan her actions. She needed to be secure within herself first about her feelings, her needs and her desires before she could choose a healthy course of action. This model gave her a chance to do just that.

EMPOWERMENT ACTION PLANNING

To develop the process of communication one step further, she used her affirmations to declare her commitment to action in the following table. She stayed centered on her own emotions and concentrated on communicating with herself to feel in touch with her personal power, to be authentic and remain strong. As you read her words, relationships in your own life might come to mind, and perhaps her example will be helpful for you to understand your personal relationship and communication needs.

SAMPLE EMPOWERING COMMUNICATION: *Relationship Issue*

Identity **I AM**	Authenticity **I NEED**	Vision **I WANT**	Action **I WILL**
Discover "Who I AM" Trust Your Truth	Declare What You NEED Speak Your Truth	Know What You WANT Create Your Vision	Commit to Action Be Willing to Live Your Truth
I am a loving woman. I am a good partner. I am affectionate and caring.	I need to feel connected and valued in my relationship. I need quality time together. I need strong communication with my partner. I need trust and honest, open commitment from my partner.	I want quality time with my partner. I want to share communication activities, passion with my husband. I want to enrich my life with interests outside of my marriage.	I will share my needs and my vision with my partner. I will improve my communication skills. I will pursue new activities to share with my husband. I will enhance my own life so that I have interests outside of my marriage.

Later, she used the same format to initiate a conversation with her spouse. Their discussion was free of blame and expectations. It is important to remember that when engaged in a conversation with an individual, you must not assume what he or she wants or needs, nor should you have expectations of him or her before or during the discussion.

An expectation (internal self-talk) is often a form of "pre-meditated resentment," and we should avoid setting ourself up for disappointment. What we can have, as a result of an empowering conversation, is an *agreement*. An agreement is a much healthier form of communication. Agreements involve others, necessitate effective dialogue, and can lead to more fulfilling outcomes because they are rooted in purposeful action that is aligned with our authenticity and vision.

If you would like to have an empowering conversation with your partner, I recommend that you first use this format with yourself to gain clarity about who you are, what you bring to the relationship, and what you need from your partner. Ask yourself what is your vision for the relationship and what actions you are willing to commit to in order to achieve fulfillment. Once you have these answers, you can then engage with your spouse or partner to share your insights.

After communicating your answers to the I AM / I NEED / I WANT / I WILL model, it is a good idea to ask open-ended or reflective questions to see what your partner feels about what you have said. Questions like: *What do you think about what I shared? What thoughts or questions do you have? How do you feel about my vision for us?* If possible, ask your spouse to share his or her needs or vision for your relationship. *Invite* him or her to share, but don't demand or force a discussion of feelings.

With timing and the right sensitivity, you will hopefully create an opportunity for the two of you to explore a shared vision, discuss how you might better meet each other's needs, and ultimately you will be able to reach agreement on what you are willing to do in joint commitment to the relationship.

EMPOWERING EMPLOYEES

Professional managers have also used this empowering conversation model to engage in conversation with their employees. It is an effective communication vehicle that facilitates the process of getting to know each other. Managers have followed this format to:

- Communicate goals and expectations to direct reports
- Assess an employee's willingness to work toward a shared vision
- Help employees identify developmental needs
- Encourage individuals to ask for help with their professional needs

The following scenario diagrams the conversation model of a new manager who was getting to know his team. He was interested in communicating his expectations to his employees, and he wanted to assess their willingness to commit to roles and responsibilities. He had only been in his role three months, but he knew all of his direct reports from having worked with them previously for a number of years.

To begin, he used "I" statements as a way of expressing his own priorities and needs. He shared his vision as well as his intention of helping the employees achieve their visions. The model was intended to be used as a two-way dialogue, and the manager was encouraged to share his thoughts about each employee before they were asked to respond with their own "I" statements. As outlined below, in addition to asking each employee for their commitment to action, the manager shared his own pledge of support to help each employee develop to maximum potential.

The empowerment conversation allows you, the organizational leader, to begin with positive statements or affirmations about your values, your gifts and your vision. With positive affirmation of your innate qualities, strengths and past performance, it is easier to identify and embrace developmental needs. Awareness of strengths and needs will allow you (and others) to feel whole and is also a prerequisite for action.

SAMPLE EMPOWERING COMMUNICATION: *Employee Conversation*

Identity **I AM**	Authenticity **I NEED**	Vision **I WANT**	Action **I WILL**
Discover "Who I AM" Trust Your Truth	Declare What You NEED Speak Your Truth	Know What You WANT Create Your Vision	Commit to Action Be Willing to Live Your Truth
Describe yourself to each employee. You might say: I am hardworking, committed to a strong team, detail-oriented, a high achiever, etc.	You state what you NEED from each person on your team. You could discuss what you NEED in terms of his or her job responsibilities.	State your overall VISION for the team. You might say: I want to support my team's growth; I want great feedback from others about our team; I want each of you to enjoy working here.	State what you WILL DO to make that vision happen. State the ACTIONS you will take to support your team. What will you do to help them so you can achieve your shared vision?
Use this table to dialog with each person. State your thoughts first, and then invite your employee to do the same. You could list an employee's strengths because that starts you off on a positive note. Or he or she can present his or her own ideas. I AM is really a statement of strengths.	You ask your employee What He Needs (from you) to grow professionally or to be successful.	Ask your employee what her VISION is. Does her VISION for the team match *yours*? If not, there is a discrepancy that needs to be discussed.	Here is where your employee commits to ACTION. You can ask him to commit to certain actions, behaviors, expectations such as: punctuality, getting work done as requested, dressing appropriately, or other work-related items that are part of roles and responsibilities.

EMPOWERMENT CONVERSATION: *Your Personal Worksheet*

Below is a template that you can use for your own empowerment conversations. This worksheet can help you sort out your emotions and enable you to better understand the beliefs that may be limiting your potential. Use this model whenever you need to assess how you are feeling as it relates to what you are doing, or not doing, in pursuit of your goals. In addition, you may choose to use it as an outline to help you prepare for an empowering conversation with another person.

FACT	
EMOTION	
EMOTIONAL NEED	
LIMITING BELIEF	
TURN-AROUND STATEMENT	
SYMBOLIC ACTION	

*You may develop a purposeful symbolic action that helps reinforce and practice your new belief or you may shift to the Empowerment Action Planning exercise on the next page.

On the next page you will find an Empowerment Action Planning worksheet. You may wish to review the examples on the previous pages as you think about situations in your life that might benefit from an empowering conversation technique. This model has been successfully used with employees by organizational leaders to secure shared responsibility and commitment to action and to help employees understand their roles and job responsibilities. It has also been utilized by entrepreneurs and professionals (such as interior designers, writers and consultants) to engage in a productive conversation with clients that would lead to mutual agreement, a shared vision, and a commitment to action.

EMPOWERMENT ACTION PLANNING

Identity **I AM**	Authenticity **I NEED**	Vision **I WANT**	Action **I WILL**
Discover "Who I AM" Trust Your Truth	Declare What You NEED Speak Your Truth	Know What You WANT Create Your Vision	Commit to Action Be Willing to Live Your Truth
Create affirmations that reinforce who you are:	Create affirmations that declare what you need to be authentic:	Create affirmations that state your vision and the highest ideal for what you want in your life:	

* May be followed by a purposeful symbolic action that helps reinforce and practice your new belief.

CIRCLE OF COMMUNICATION

As we have seen with Empowerment Conversations, communication is a valuable tool for helping us hold our place of power. It is the means by which we are able live authentically, sharing and affirming our values, wants and needs. It is the thread that weaves relationships together. When we communicate we link our internal thoughts to our outward expressions. Knowing this, I developed a model to facilitate the exchange of thoughts and ideas. To me, communication is a pre-requisite for action.

The Circle of Communication model enhances our ability to effectively communicate our vision to ourselves and others. It is designed to help create awareness of individual commitment and goals. This instrument can be used to identify opportunities for development and to build an action plan for achieving the desired vision.

CIRCLE OF COMMUNICATION

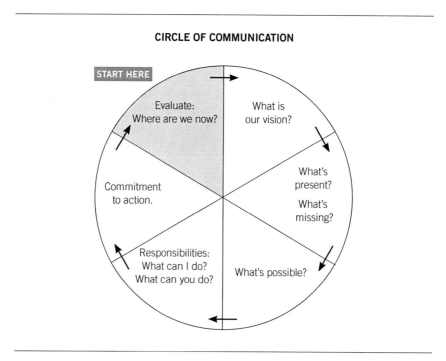

The Circle framework is based on the Mobius Model™ which was developed in 1991 by Dr. Will Stockton. The original model was designed to help facilitate commitment to team goals and values and to identify resources for implementing a committed action plan. It is an ideal methodology for individuals, partners or teams to facilitate productive conversation, and the circular format allows for continuous evaluation and assessment of progress against goals.

Clients have used the Circle model to develop their entrepreneurial vision and evaluate potential business opportunities. Professional and executive clients have used this exercise to engage employees in the process of creating a shared vision, formulating action plans, and assigning tasks. As you might imagine, the circle of communication is an effective vehicle for facilitating a discussion in personal relationships as well.

The Circle of Communication diagram is self-explanatory: Begin at the starting point. Evaluate the present situation, and then continue with the motion of the wheel to define a vision and to evaluate what's already in place and what is needed to achieve that vision. "What's present?" encourages positive thinking first before one looks at "What's missing?" The questions "What's possible?" or "What are the opportunities?" provide an opening to brainstorm and think outside of the box to create potential ideas, different solutions and various outcomes.

When an individual uses the model alone, "Responsibilities" may just be a listing of all of the things that have to get done to accomplish a primary goal. Or responsibilities could include intermediate steps needed to crystallize a final vision. Perhaps it may be necessary to involve others in the exploration. Some responsibilities or ideas (developed in the brainstorming phase) can be delegated.

Clarifying shared responsibilities and assigning specific tasks is important when the circle of communication process involves (business or relationship) partners and teams. The questions "What can I do?" and "What can you do?" empower everyone to participate and to concentrate on doing those things that align with individual strengths and capabilities.

The last critical step in the circle involves setting forth a commitment to action. This may involve a timeline of activities or a prioritization of things to do. This segment of the circle can be customized to individual and team needs. What is most important is to establish clear objectives and measurable action items against which one can evaluate progress against goals.

Finally, the circle progression returns to the starting position, at which point the process begins again – evaluation through commitment to action. The process can be repeated as often as necessary to develop and refine action steps to fulfill a desired vision.

LINKS TO POTENTIAL

A valuable resource is listed below.

The Mobius Model™ *A Guide for Developing Effective Relationships in Groups, Teams, and Organizations* by Larry Demarest, Ph.D., Marjorie Herdes, Joyce Stockton, Ph.D., and William Stockton, Ph.D.

ACTION EXERCISES

In its most descriptive connotation, *action* means achievement. To achieve your potential, in part, is to accomplish or complete a goal. Goals, by definition, are the visions toward which you progress. Therefore, your vision supersedes your actions. Vision can feed your soul with purposeful energy. Actions are the final step in becoming sentient.

You have gained awareness of your values, gifts, strengths and emotional needs; you have prepared yourself for living authentically; and you have discovered and developed your visions for the future. Now you are ready for the last part of your journey toward fulfilling your potential: *Your commitment to action.*

As you contemplate your visions and the actions to which you must commit, you should begin with the end in mind. That said, ask yourself "what is my life purpose?" Transcend the practicalities of everyday living, and search for deeper wisdom concerning your existence.

Ask yourself: "What lessons am I meant to learn, and what contributions am I destined to make during my life on Earth?" Look deep within yourself. Touch that sacred, spiritual place within your heart. Feel the essence of your soul, and embrace your higher purpose.

To help you discover your soul purpose and grow as a spiritual being, fast-forward your mind to the end of your life. What would a final tribute say if you lived your life with purpose? What would you have accomplished that would be noteworthy enough to write about in your obituary?

The following is a sample life tribute to read in preparation for writing your own. As you consider the story of Jill James, a woman who lived her passions and dreams, think about your own life and how you would like to be remembered. Notice that Ms. James successfully developed and achieved her life vision within the context of her greatest potential. From her example, we learn that reaching one's potential is the highest form of achievement. In essence, inherent in this achievement of potential is not only success but real life fulfillment.

TRIBUTE TO JILL JAMES

Jill James, an advocate for ethical medical treatment for all people, used her own personal tragedy to help transform medical ethics law. She pioneered advancements in health care delivery that benefited all people, regardless of ability to pay. James – who suffered the loss of her own child from a rare form of heart disease – worked for many years to support all people in need of medical treatment and organ transplantation. Born in Minneapolis to Robert and Kathryn James, a physician and a nurse practitioner, she grew up with a loving model of service to the community. She died from respiratory failure April 3 at Minneapolis Medical Center after a long illness.

Ms. James attended Mount Holyoke College where she received a Bachelor of Science in Education. She later attended the University of Minnesota where she received her MBA as well as her law degree. She practiced law for a short time with the Ford Law Firm before venturing out on her own. James was an active community volunteer. She spearheaded the innovative construction of a community hospital focused on maternal and child health. She was elected Board Chair of the Babies & Children's Foundation after raising $20 million for the institution.

She was an accomplished public speaker who engaged audiences throughout the state, highlighting the issues affecting lower income families. Her outspoken, yet well-respected, opinions brought her to the Governor's office where she became the Advisor for Human Welfare and Social Justice. Her appearances before the legislature helped reform medical insurance practices throughout the region.

A gourmet cook who loved entertaining, Jill taught cooking classes for young women in her home and cherished the idea of bringing "old school" domestic practices into the lives of busy professionals. She created and financed the Jill James European Scholarship of the Culinary Institute of America, a fund that offered women the opportunity to spend two weeks in France studying under some of the world's finest chefs.

Despite an extremely busy professional career, Jill's family was her most important priority. The mother of four children and grandmother of 10, James reveled in all family celebrations. To celebrate her 75th birthday, she traveled to France with her children and grandchildren where they stayed at the world-renowned Chateau Magnifique in the heart of the Loire Valley.

Jill's life revolved around loving others and sharing her passion with the world around her. The memorial service celebrating Jill's life included exotic flowers from California and Hawaii, a gourmet buffet presented by past recipients of the Jill James Scholarship Fund, and special reserve wine from her beloved Kathryn Vineyard, which she founded in memory of her daughter. Memorials are preferred to the Jill James Fund of the Twin Cities Babies & Children's Foundation. Friends and family are encouraged to celebrate life by spending the day with someone they love.

EXERCISE 1: *Write Your Personal Tribute*
Now it is time for you to write your own tribute and personal reflection of your life. Think about your values and what inspires you to live a purpose-filled life. In preparing your tribute consider these questions:

1. What accomplishments or measurable events must occur during your lifetime so that you will consider your life to have been satisfying and well-lived?

2. What does living a life with few or no regrets mean to you?

3. What is your greatest passion?

4. How do you achieve fulfillment with enthusiasm and joyfulness?

5. What words best describe your character, your relationships and your accomplishments?

6. What does "community" mean to you? How do you help your community?

7. What is your relationship with your Higher Power? How do you serve others in the context of a Universal order?

8. What distinct gifts do you bring to this world as an individual with a unique and special purpose?

YOUR PERSONAL TRIBUTE

_____

_____

_____

_____

_____

_____

_____

_____

_____

_____

_____

_____

_____

_____

_____

_____

_____

_____

_____

_____

_____

_____

_____

_____

_____

_____

EXERCISE 2: *Personal Mission Statement*

By writing your personal tribute, you will know how you want to feel about your life when it is over. Now that you have articulated what accomplishments would be most meaningful to achieve, it is time to craft a personal mission statement for how you are going to live your life from this moment forward. A personal mission statement incorporates both your values and vision, and it can become a statement of intent and desire.

Writing a mission statement is a long-standing, well-accepted practice. All successful organizations have mission statements. They create strategic plans and corporate objectives in accordance with their mission and vision. Then they can move forward with purposeful action. Individuals have adopted the practice of writing personal mission statements to help them focus on their highest priorities and to stay on their journey for greater personal and professional fulfillment.

By writing a personal statement, you can focus on your higher purpose. Composing a personal mission statement that incorporates your vision and values will allow you to gain a blueprint for aligning your daily actions with the things you value most. A personal mission statement will improve your ability to achieve your goals.

Sample Mission Statements

"I will live my life with integrity and authenticity. I will nurture and cherish my children and grandchildren with a loving heart. I will use my innate gifts to passionately explore my life opportunities. I will be generous and demonstrate caring by serving others with compassion. I will trust in my higher power as I strive for a life of fulfillment."

"I will use my natural creative gifts to beautify the world and bring joy into the lives of others. I will express my passion and love of life through my artwork, my music, and my writing. I will commit to helping those less fortunate than myself by volunteering my time and donating my artistic efforts to community organizations. I will work toward preserving the earth's natural resources and protecting the environment in all that I do."

A comprehensive personal mission statement is derived through self-awareness. Throughout this book, you have been engaged in a carefully articulated process of gaining self-awareness. To develop a mission statement, you may wish to revisit the values exercise completed earlier in this book, or you may choose a quiet time of reflection about your vision for the future. The personal tribute that you have just created may also be helpful as a catalyst for crafting your personal mission statement.

YOUR PERSONAL MISSION STATEMENT

LIFE PATH: *Reflections and Understanding*

Before you begin building a life plan, it is helpful to look at how your life journey has unfolded thus far. This will help you understand the natural patterns of your life and give you a picture of your journey's ebb and flow to date. The Life Path exercise is used to illustrate the non-linear nature of life, and it gives you an opportunity to assess what events have influenced who and where you are today.

LIFE PATH

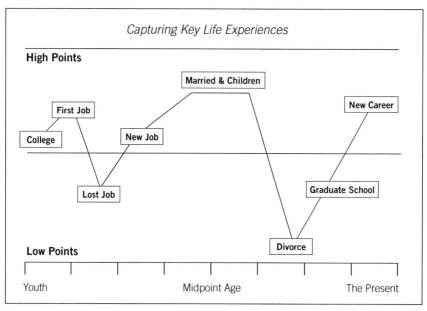

Capturing Key Life Experiences

High Points

Married & Children
First Job
New Career
College
New Job
Lost Job
Graduate School
Divorce

Low Points

Youth   Midpoint Age   The Present

As seen in the sample Life Path shown above, you will use this exercise to record events that are memorable to you. These experiences will appear as points along a continuum. You will begin at the left of the central lifeline and indicate key experiences from childhood to the present time. All important occasions or significant episodes should be represented to help define your life's pattern.

To do this exercise, ask yourself to think about each major event of your life and assess whether you would consider it a high point or a low point. Was the experience joyful and celebratory, or was it challenging and difficult? Was there a special occasion that changed your life? What episodes in your personal life, relationships and career are memorable and significant enough to be recorded on your life path?

Carefully place key events and life experiences on your Life Path in terms of how they are remembered: High, Neutral or Low. Evaluate and record the differences between each event in your mind. Note the sequence and flow of your experiences. Overall has your life been measured and remembered "above the line," or have you had more episodes and events "below" the line? Have you seen a pattern of ups and downs, or has your life been more of an even-keeled stream of events?

Most of us have experienced at least some significant highs and lows in our lifetime. As you reflect on this unique view of your life journey, note what characteristics were prevalent during your high points. At these moments in your life, how were your emotional needs being met? What did the low points in your life have in common? What behavioral patterns did you develop to help you move up from the low points? When were you most aligned with your values and life purpose? And finally, look at where you are now. Your present situation is not an end point but, rather, a starting point for your journey toward your vision and life fulfillment.

EXERCISE 3: *Draw Your Life Path*

Capturing Key Life Experiences

High Points

Low Points

| Youth | | | | Midpoint Age | | | The Present |

Journey of Discovery. Let's stop for a moment and assess where you are now: You began with the end in mind and composed a **Personal Tribute**. You used this life reflection to envision what you would like your ultimate life achievements to be. This exercise allowed you to express your life purpose and to remind you of those actions which would be most important and synonymous with your values.

You then crafted a **Personal Mission Statement** to reinforce your vision and allow you to focus on your higher purpose. The intent here was to compose a personal mission statement that incorporated your vision and values and set out a blueprint for guiding your daily actions to include the things you value most.

And lastly, you charted your **Life Path**, an exercise designed to illustrate the non-linear nature of life. You accentuated the highs and lows of your accomplishments and life challenges, studied the relationship of these significant events to your values and behaviors, and assessed how they correlate with the fulfillment of your emotional needs. You have created an outline for understanding the natural rhythm of your life: what sustains you at your highest point, and what has propelled you to move up from the depths of your challenges.

You have looked forward to your ideal vision, and you looked back at the events of your life up to this moment. And now, you have arrived at the moment when life offers you the greatest gift: the ***Present!***

The present is not an end point but, rather, a starting point for the continuation of your journey. You are prepared to pursue your vision. You are well-positioned for creating a life of fulfillment. It is time to commit to **Action**.

Earlier in this chapter, we defined **Action** as "purposeful, deliberate progress…to take steps and proceed." Sounds simple, doesn't it? Well, creating the life you want and achieving your vision really is that simple! If you have done the exercises outlined in this book, then you have all the knowledge that you need to move forward. You have affirmed your gifts and acknowledged that you can achieve your goals. You have the knowledge; now you need the action plan. Abu Bakr, the Prophet Mohammed's closest companion and adviser once said, **"Without knowledge, action is useless, and knowledge without action is futile."**

At this moment on your journey, you know where you are (The Present), and you know where you want to be (Your Vision). Furthermore, your Life Path diagram illustrates that life, as you know it, is not likely a straight line. On the contrary, most life journeys involve experiencing peaks and valleys. There is a tender balance – a delicate relationship – between your intentions and actual outcomes.

Life involves an integration of scientific and spiritual principles. Our existence includes both a metaphysical and physical reality. When we take internal control of our life with a definitive purposeful plan, we must also pay attention to the external feedback we receive. It is possi-

Being present in the moment suggests that "the time is now."

ble that unplanned influences that come into our life may offer us greater potential if we choose to follow where they lead. Metaphysical philosophy teaches us to: *Hold firm to the impulse of our desire but let the form (or outcome) be flexible.*

Even as you plan your actions to advance toward your future, pay particular attention to the present moment. If need be, listen to the quiet of silence, close your eyes, and take a deep breath. Appreciate the power of your existence. Know that each moment only happens once in a lifetime. Take in its beauty, and rejoice in the fact that you have arrived at this point in time. Only when you allow yourself to truly experience the universal spirit of each moment can you invite the metaphysical laws of attraction to support you on your journey.

Being present in the moment also suggests that "the time is now" – a time to throw off the shackles of your past. It is a time to focus positively on your vision for the future. Your vision is what gives you hope, meaning, direction, and a way to measure your progress. However, it is purposeful action toward that vision that frees you from the bonds of your past.

Many people tend to live their life with the belief that they **alone** must "make it happen." Making life happen requires a vision, plan, support system and courage. It also requires purposeful action. We are empowered to be in control. We can control our efforts, but we can't always control the outcome. Individuals need to temper their "need to control" enough to allow the external world to respond to their energy.

You can still work hard. You can still be achievement-oriented, and you can set definitive plans to pursue your goals. In the final analysis, you take purposeful action, and you need to allow the Universe to present opportunities for your life. In so doing, you will *make it happen* and *let it happen* when you live in the present moment.

ACTION PLANNING

In combination, the words *Action* and *Planning* present a dichotomy. To succeed, you actually need both elements in your life – you need to plan, and you need to act on your plan. Some *planning* enthusiasts would argue that best results come when you spend 80 percent of your time planning and only 20 percent of your time actively working your plan. You may have developed and implemented different plans in both your personal life and in your professional career – strategic, business, marketing, and financial plans. While there is inherent value in creating each type of plan, it is important to find the delicate balance between the act of planning and purposefully taking real *action.*

For some, the planning phase can be cumbersome and overwhelming. If you are not careful, you may submerge yourself writing such detailed, all-inclusive plans that you never take a definitive step forward. "Over planning" is akin to what some call "analysis paralysis." I know because I once spent nearly a year creating and revising an exhaustive 12-page marketing plan. The result of my effort was a just that: a 12-page plan. I never pushed myself away from the computer long enough to act on my plan! I thought my plan had to be perfect. Well, it turned out to be perfectly useless! So, I caution you (from personal experience) to balance your need for creating a planned, structured and tactical approach with getting out there and *just doing it*!

Balancing action and planning can offer you a greater sense of accomplishment and fulfillment. I have synthesized an approach to this that resembles an elementary concept: the daily lesson plan. And it works! This method will allow you to hold firm to the dream of achieving your vision, to affirm yourself in the process of daily living, and to take definitive steps toward your goal.

My entrepreneur coach and friend, Mark LeBlanc, author of the best-selling book Growing Your Business, has trained thousands of business owners nationwide in what they need to *know* and what they need to *do* to start and grow their business. He recommends asking yourself every morning "What am I going to do today to bring me closer to my goal?"

Since meeting Mark several years ago, I have concentrated on choosing three action items every day to move me forward. This approach is simple and has a great multiplier effect: three activities per day times 30 days per month means that every month I have accomplished 90 tasks toward my goal. In a given year, that monthly average translates to more than 1,000 annual productive (and completed) activities!

You may also love this system because it allows you to feel a sense of accomplishment each and every day without feeling overwhelmed or intimidated by an insurmountable list of things to do. Using this process, write the three things that you want to complete into your daily calendar on your desk or computer. You may want to allow your computer's alarm system to remind you that these are action steps, or goals, that you want to accomplish. This system is affectionately called: **To Do and Ta Da!** Each morning you will know what you have to do, and each evening, when you see what you have done, you can celebrate your accomplishments with a triumphant: **Ta Da!**

In conclusion, I want to encourage you to practice four essentials for achieving a life of fulfillment: *focus, dedication, a sense of purpose and faith.*

Focus on your vision and what you intend to achieve. The magnetic nature of your vision should pull you out of bed each morning. The visceral sense of exhilaration when you think about achieving your vision is what will propel you forward even if the movement is miniscule or equivalent to a baby's first steps. Be willing to get up each day and try. Benjamin Disraeli proclaimed that "Action may not always bring happiness; but there is no happiness without action."

Focus your attention in the direction of your highest ideal. Focus on affirming yourself with daily declarations of your natural gifts. Daily affirmations will help you stay focused in the direction of your dreams. Affirmations need not be complex; on the contrary, *Say Something Simple!* Remember, your daily affirmation is meant to help you radiate positive energy. Energy is the dynamic force in the law of attraction.

Your energy will naturally arise from your passion if your vision is borne from your deepest desire. Napoleon Hill, the great American author, wisely states, "Desire is the starting point of all achievement, not a hope, not a wish, but a keen pulsating desire which transcends everything. Create a definite plan for carrying out your desire and begin at once, whether you are ready or not, to put this plan into action."

Dedicate yourself to your highest priorities to ensure that you take action every day! Be sure that you don't confuse activity with achievement. Choose actions that will bring you one step closer to your goal. Trust yourself in knowing the difference between "busy work" and productive work. Your values will influence your daily choices and guide you toward appropriate activity. No matter what you choose to do, live each moment with a **sense of purpose** because as Lao Tse said, "Your actions are your only possessions."

And finally, have **faith**. You are a unique individual with a lifetime opportunity to embrace your authentic self and to realize your potential. At the moment of your birth, you embarked on a lifelong journey of discovery. And now, as you continue on your path, remember you have many choices, great possibility, and immense power to achieve your dreams. Each step you take is an opportunity to further your awareness and enhance your personal growth. May your journey lead you to a sentient life, one that offers you contentment, inner peace, and the Promise of your Potential.

Links to Potential

Other valuable resources are listed below.

- *Seven Habits of Highly Effective People* by Stephen Covey
  www.FranklinCovey.com

- *Small Business Success* by Mark LeBlanc
  www.SmallBusinessSuccess.com

APPENDIX

Partners in Power

Being authentic, making the necessary choices to achieve your goals, and following through on your commitment to action require self-esteem and confidence. Building confidence is a gradual process requiring energy and consistency for the sustenance of physical and emotional health. While building confidence is an internal process, one that must emanate from our core being, there are several ways to strengthen and reinforce self-esteem. There are different ways to nourish ourselves and sustain the energy we need for personal growth. I call these sources of support for our well-being *Partners in Power*. These sources of energy that support our growth process include:

Physical
- Healthy nutrition
- Rest and relaxation
- Physical exercise (energy release or time with nature)

Spiritual
- Meditation or Spiritual Connection
- Intuition (Trusting our Truth)

Social
- Individual Support System (intimate relationships, family and close friends)
- Personal advocates, coaches and mentors

Our *Partners in Power* are important because they energize us and feed our development. They add nourishment to our physical and emotional health to help sustain positive feelings. Just like the self-affirmations used in *Coaching to the Core* to build and maintain confidence, individuals need to utilize their *Partners in Power* on a daily process. These sources of energy are the nutrients for the physical, spiritual and social health needed for the intellectual process of growth.

When you go through growth periods, you need more energy to sustain your growth – you need to nourish yourself. If you don't add nourishment, your energy can get depleted, and you may revert back to old behaviors and thought processes. When your energy is low, there can be an adverse effect on your emotions and attitude. This may be especially true for you when you are very tired or stressed. You may notice a drop in your physical energy, and it may be harder to think encouraging thoughts.

Think about what energizes you and what helps create your sense of internal well-being. Some people need a healthy well-balanced diet and the proper rest to feel energized, physically fit and mentally astute. Some feel sluggish from too many carbohydrates, and with too much fat or sugar mental acuity suffers. Conversely, when a person has a good night's sleep and eats the proper food for maintaining optimum weight, he or she feels revitalized and mentally charged. Physical exercise – whether it be an aerobic workout or a brisk walk/jog in the fresh air, also stimulates positive feelings and vibrant energy.

Perhaps you need quiet rest and relaxation to center your thoughts and focus your energy. Meditation with candles and soft peaceful music may help you gain a spiritual connection. With quiet and solitude, you might be best able to tap into your intuition. Trusting your inner truth is a powerful tool that reinforces the confidence you have gained through self-awareness.

Of course, there may be other times when you seek the comfort and counsel of close friends to fortify your thought process. Personal advocates who share your commitment to personal growth and achievement help diffuse the demons of self-doubt when you might be overtired or stressed. Perhaps when you are in the midst of a "growth spurt," friends and family may offer valuable reassurance as you examine old beliefs and "try on" new behaviors.

Personal advocates, coaches and mentors, as people who care about you, are valuable *Partners in Power*. They present special opportunities to augment your growth when they reach out to offer help in support of your development. Reaching out to them does not diminish your power. On the contrary, it enhances it. Knowing *when* and *how* to ask for help and being able to accept it are all part of being an empowered individual.

COACHES

Coaching can be a powerful alliance designed to enhance personal development and lifelong learning. Professional coaches serve as cheerleaders, sounding boards, confidants, resources and advocates for their clients. An executive coach or a life coach can be a valuable resource if the coach empowers you to look internally for the answers that will strengthen your confidence.

An effective coach recognizes that the client is naturally creative, resourceful and whole. There is nothing wrong with the client that the coach needs to focus on or "fix." On the contrary, the client sets the goals and objectives for coaching, and the relationship focuses on helping the client get the results that he or she most desires. An effective coach will partner with each client to *ask the questions* knowing that the *client has the answers*. A skilled coach ensures that the client stays centered on the path toward fulfillment and life balance.

With regular and consistent sessions, the coach can help the client apply the coaching lessons to daily work and life situations. A good coach has been trained in both listening and questioning techniques. The coach's role is to listen, to ask the client penetrating questions to create more self-awareness, and to deepen the learning by holding the client accountable for movement toward desired goals. Some coaches have a highly developed intuition, and they will apply their insight to offer clients a broader perspective beyond what is seen and heard from mere questions and answers.

Coaches who employ value-based coaching techniques encourage clients to integrate their own values into their relationships and life decisions. To illustrate, take for example, Jack, an experienced sales professional who hired a coach at a critical time in his career:

Jack had a fabulous professional track record – 10 years as a seasoned sales executive. He not only enjoyed selling executive education services but was extremely successful and respected by his peers and others in the industry. During the technology "boom" in the year 2000, Jack was recruited (along with 10 other savvy salespeople) to join a fast-paced, high-tech start-up company selling Web-based services.

Within the first nine months with the company, Jack and the other 10 new sales people began to doubt the company's ability to follow through on the technology solutions that they were positioned to sell. By the end of the first year, half of the sales executives had left the company or were fired for nonperformance. Jack was one of five people still employed. None of them was meeting sales quotas, and in light of the circumstances, Jack became anxious, his confidence was shaken, and he began doubting his abilities. The recruiter who placed Jack (and two other sales executives at the company) was aware of the challenges, and she really cared about Jack, so she encouraged him to get a coach to sort through his emotions and his difficulties at work.

Jack's coach began the partnership by asking him about his priorities. *What did he hope to accomplish by engaging in a coaching partnership?* Jack was very clear: he wanted to achieve greater fulfillment in his career. He anticipated he would have to leave his current position but was insecure about how to go about making that change.

The coach used a values exercise (similar to the one presented in this book) to get to know Jack better and to build a foundation for the coaching partnership. A few weeks later, Jack and his coach discussed Jack's values and his options for moving forward in his career. It had become clear that he wanted *and needed* to leave his current job, but he was unprepared to make the "how and when" decisions without help from his coach.

Using a straightforward questioning technique, Jack's coach asked him to brainstorm ideas or options for how he might leave the company. Jack came up with three ideas:

1. He could wait until he was given the 30-day notice to improve his performance, just like several of his peers. This would buy him some time to look for another job. In essence, he would "fail" in this job but gain time to leverage a new opportunity.

2. He could approach his boss' manager and describe how inequitable, unethical and biased she had been in dealing with him during the course of the last six months. He would state a case for discrimination (based on age) because he was the oldest sales person on the force. He would hopefully gain compensation and quiet encouragement for his decision to leave the company.

3. He could talk to management and be honest that things were not working out for him at the company. While he knew he had the talent and could perform, he felt the company would be better served by someone whose passion and skill set was better aligned with the company's philosophies. He could approach management with a win-win formula saying something like: "Let's strike a deal that gives me time to find something else and you (the company) a solid transition plan for my active accounts."

His coach listened to all of the options and asked just one question: "Jack, which one of these is most aligned with your values?" Hands down, Jack was a negotiator and peaceful resolution maker – the third option was his first (and ONLY) choice if he stayed true to his values. Most of Jack's friends thought he was crazy to think a company would pay him to leave. In the end, with coaching support, Jack did negotiate a severance package for leaving the company by quitting. His coach kept him focused on his values and his vision. He was able to transition out of the job with a month's pay to help prepare him to search for and identify other opportunities more aligned with his talents, emotional needs and career vision.

Coaching partnerships center on the client's whole life. Achieving life balance in all parts of one's life – career, money, family, friends, health, recreation and spirituality – is important for emotional and physical well-being. Sometimes, when a coach is working with a client to effect change in one area of life, challenges may surface in another area. Dave, a manager at a home remodeling company, was working with a coach to improve his time-management skills. He wanted to be more effective and productive at work so his boss would consider promoting him and adding to his responsibilities.

As Dave and his coach assessed how he spent his time each day, it became clear that while he valued his relationship with his wife and children, he was spending more and more time at the office. As his workday got longer, his personal time at home got shorter, and his relationships suffered. Because he became more aware of his values and priorities through his coaching conversations, Dave discovered this imbalance. He acknowledged that there was unspoken tension at home, and his coach provided the insight that this constant tension was also interfering with his productivity at work.

So while the goal for coaching began with a career time-management objective, the coach worked with Dave on improving his situation at home first. She encouraged him to use the empowering conversation model (I am / I need / I want / I will) to initiate a conversation with his wife. He outlined what he was hoping to accomplish with this exercise:

- He wanted to share his goals at work with his wife so she could have a better appreciation for his career (*I am* working hard to hopefully get a promotion).

- He needed her support (*I need* my family to understand and support me).

- He wanted to openly discuss the vision for a more balanced lifestyle between work and home. He hoped that his wife would share the vision (*I want* to improve my work schedule and learn more effective ways to spend my time AND I want the quality of my time at home to be more enjoyable and satisfying for everyone).

- He was willing to discuss ideas to create ways for both of them to achieve their vision (*I will* do whatever we agree to do in support of these goals).

Dave's coach encouraged him to be open to hearing his wife's needs and to working with her to formulate a vision of what they both wanted. It turned out that she was very receptive to the conversation, and together they came up with a clever and valuable solution. Since Dave was working so hard, he was also not getting the exercise he needed. His wife felt she didn't have time to talk to him about her life either.

So Dave and his wife committed to using the first 30 minutes of time when he came home each night to walk and to talk about their respective days. They agreed to take the walk no matter what time Dave got home. They started the plan in early June, and the entire summer they had fun planning the excursions (sometimes they would even walk to a local restaurant for dinner). Often they ended up spending even more time walking together because they were invigorated by the exercise or their conversation.

Dave's coach helped keep him accountable to his plan, and she worked with him on how to improve the structure of his day at the office so he could be more productive and still leave the office at a reasonable time each night. Because of his brisk evening walks with his wife, Dave felt healthier, slept better, and his energy increased during the business day. The coaching partnership was extremely valuable for Dave because it successfully addressed challenges at both work and home, helping him create more balance and fulfillment in his whole life.

Most coaches require more than a three-month commitment when working with a new client. Change happens over time, and many coaches want to see their clients sustain the change while they are held accountable to new behavior patterns developed during coaching. Sometimes a coach may be a valuable resource during a transitional period, and the engagement may not last the full three months. Mattie is a good example of a short-term but productive coaching client.

Mattie was about 12 years into her career as a manager in a turbulent, highly competitive industry – cable TV. Her company was experiencing heavy competition from alternative sources for home television service, and it needed to cut costs and lower consumer prices to compete more effectively. Mattie was one of the middle-managers laid off suddenly. The economy was in a slump, the job market was very tight, and Mattie had not worked outside the cable TV industry, so she was scared and insecure about finding another job. Furthermore, her confidence had been shaken when she was laid off without notice even though her performance had always been rated very high.

Mattie decided to hire someone to help her rewrite her resumé. She was referred to a woman who worked with many individuals in the midst of career transitions. This woman's services included: resumé writing, job search and networking strategies, and interviewing skills. She had been trained as a professional coach who also used visioning techniques as part of the process to help clients articulate what type of job they most desired.

When Mattie first met with her coach, she was surprised that she needed a full coaching session just to request help with her resumé. The coach knew that it was imperative to spend adequate time with Mattie to appreciate her values and vision – together with her career experience – in order to write an effective resumé that captured her best qualities. As part of their initial meeting, her coach uncovered Mattie's insecurity and lack of confidence about her abilities. The coach recognized that no matter how well the resumé was written, under the present circumstances Mattie would not interview with passion and confidence to authentically represent the positive achievements and skills listed on her resumé.

Mattie agreed to work with the coach for one month, meeting once a week to initiate a four-part strategy. Under their agreement, Mattie would:

1. Work with the coach to identify her values and personal characteristics about which she felt most proud. She would describe in detail all accomplishments and skills that she had exemplified throughout her career.

2. Research job postings and ads that described positions of interest to her even if she did not feel she was qualified for the specific job. She would underline or highlight any part of the description that was something she knew she could do effectively. Mattie's coach also would work with her during these sessions to appreciate skills that could transfer outside of her industry. As part of this process, her coach would gather the necessary information to redraft Mattie's resumé; she would incorporate Mattie's accomplishments and link them to job opportunities and target organizations where she felt there would be a good fit.

3. Use one complete session to engage with her coach in a vision exercise that formulated her highest vision. The vision would include a full description of the skills she would be using, the environment in which she would work, the types of people with whom she would be involved, her compensation and rewards, and any other details that would be appealing in an ideal situation.

4. Implement a networking strategy to which she would be held accountable. The plan included scheduling informational interviews and asking for referrals from a variety of sources. She would meet with as many people as possible and, as part of the strategy, her coach would help Mattie confidently articulate the professional competencies she had developed and demonstrated throughout her career. Mattie would also use her vision as a basis for describing what she most loved doing. Her enthusiasm would help her explain how she would make a significant contribution to a prospective organization.

As you might imagine, this short-term coaching exercise was extremely valuable to Mattie. Her coach was truly her *Partner in Power* as she encouraged Mattie to develop greater self-awareness and to create a vision from which she launched an enthusiastic job search for a new position. The coaching activities centered on Mattie's values and vision. Mattie did all of the work, including providing her coach the information needed to authentically represent her in the resumé. Mattie diligently worked her plan. Within three months, Mattie secured a position as a manager with a start-up organization that embraced the qualities and experience she had to offer.

As you can see from these examples, there are different reasons why people hire a coach. You may choose to use a coach as part of the process of developing your own potential. Even after reading this book, you may further benefit from the support of a coach who will help you leverage your increased self-awareness. You may like having a short-term coaching engagement to support the practice of embracing your values and vision as you advance to where you want to be. A coach won't decide *what* you want, but he or she can be instrumental in supporting *your pursuit* of what you want. By designing an alliance customized to your emotional needs, your coach can help you build the foundation for making the life changes that you have discovered you desire as a result of reading this book.

Whatever your reason for hiring a personal coach – to facilitate a life or career transition, help you lead a more balanced life, improve or enrich relationships, or start a new business venture – enjoy the gift of having a special partner in power to advocate for you and cheer you on as you progress on your journey toward fulfilling your potential.

MENTORS

Mentors, like coaches, are valuable *Partners in Power* although they are different. Both support your growth and development, but while coaches are generally trained professionals who receive pay for their services, mentors typically offer their support on a voluntary basis. Mentoring is a very old practice. This concept first appeared in Greek mythology when Odysseus, departing for the Trojan War, asked his friend Mentor to watch over his son Telemachus. Mentor safeguarded and cared for his charge. To the early Greeks, mentoring was embedded in their culture as a means to survival.

Later, mentoring emerged in guilds that taught and passed down craftsmanship to the novice. This method of mentoring has sustained itself; apprenticeships have become a valuable way to bring along a younger generation of artisans. Over the course of history, mentoring found its way into business. In its early form, mentoring was patriarchal, authoritarian and one-way. The mentor was the *guru,* and the protégé was the *sponge* – an eager learner positioned to absorb all that the wise mentor had to offer. Unfortunately, this type of partnership was highly selective. Mentors, most often white males, were actually *sponsors* who picked their young protégés – always men – based on the belief that they were younger versions of themselves. The sponsor was, in fact, choosing someone whom they could groom to sit in their own chair when they retired.

In the 21st century, with the emergence of more women and people of color in the workplace, mentoring enjoyed a resurgence, and the old model shifted. The mentoring process became more inclusive and widespread. Mentoring was everywhere…in business, in churches, the inner-city, and with the youth of our society. Ultimately, mentoring became a corporate training tool that was highly valued for its ability to develop people and promote communication, diversity, and team building.

Further, when the business world transformed through mergers and acquisitions, reorganizations, downsizing, and right-sizing, a new "employee contract" was born. There were no longer promises of "cradle-to-grave" employment, and employees were expected to take responsibility for their own development. Slowly, the corporate environment changed its approach, and mentoring became one of the fundamental ways to demonstrate how the organization valued its human assets. Embracing employees as individuals, attending to their development, and acknowledging the importance of consistent recognition emerged as cornerstones for new strategic human resource programs.

The wisest of leaders understood the correlation between humanizing the workplace and increasing an individual's ownership of the corporate mission. What they discovered is that when employees are embraced as "whole" people – people with complex needs and full lives outside of the corporate setting – there is a marked change in the quality of internal relationships, leading to an increase in retention, productivity and, ultimately, profitability. Even given the free will of employees to leave their current employer for a better "package," those companies that offer valuable programs such as mentoring enjoy greater loyalty and competitive positioning.

By the 1990s these environmental changes spawned new developmental opportunities for employees, and both formal and informal mentoring came into vogue. Many people sought out mentors in the informal sense. They looked for people who could serve as sounding boards, opinion givers, intellectual resources, and the like – people who possessed the experience or intellect to offer counsel.

Mentors can be either spontaneous or long-term. Both are valuable. People's mentors may change as their needs expand or as new phases of their life unfold. Though they may have different backgrounds, characteristics and styles, the most valuable mentors will encourage their protégé to grow. Some nudge their partner forward by raising the bar gradually; others push aggressively toward new heights. Trust is always the most essential ingredient in each partnership; only in an atmosphere of trust can the protégé welcome firm guidance, honest feedback and strong suggestions.

Just as in a coaching alliance, a mentoring partnership is a safe place to ask questions, admit developmental needs, and seek new ways to approach challenges. Interestingly, when an individual serves as a mentor, he or she may also grow and develop as part of what is called a "dynamically reciprocal" process. Sarah's story illustrates this concept.

Sarah was a volunteer mentor with an organization that matched senior executives with high-potential women in a year-long executive development program. The company was nationally recognized for its capacity to recruit executive mentors, match mentors and mentees successfully, and train all program participants to maximize the experience. Sarah was selected as a mentor because she had been an Executive Director for a nonprofit organization several years earlier. Her mentee was an extremely bright bilingual woman with two advanced degrees. For the first time in her career, Sarah's mentee Monica was serving as the Executive Director of a small nonprofit in the health care industry.

Sarah, who had never been a mentor before, entered the experience with reticence and some skepticism as to whether or not she would be a good mentor who could contribute to the development of her partner. Despite her misgivings, she participated in the mentor/mentee training and learned how to listen, ask good questions, and resist the urge to give advice. She was totally unprepared for the outgrowth of her mentoring experience.

Sarah recounted the story of sitting with her mentee, listening to Monica's self-evaluation in a performance review. She was awed by the young woman's accomplishments. In each session, she encouraged Monica to *embrace* her talents and natural abilities. Sarah was surprised by the affect of this message on her own life.

In the months that ensued, she found that by sharing her values and the core beliefs by which she lived her life, she reinforced in her own mind the principles of authenticity that guided all of her decisions. Her mentee was grateful for Sarah's genuine humility and willingness to share her valuable life experiences. As a result, Sarah gained additional confidence from the experience, strength in her leadership ability, and renewed vitality for her own career.

She was supposed to be the mentor, the one with experience, and the voice of reason! She left each session reflecting on her own strengths and abilities, her own successes, and the important principles that had served her well in her life. As a by-product of the mentoring conversations, she began listening to and heeding her own words. In the end, she felt that she had gained more than she had given in this reciprocal partnership.

In the course of my career, I have sought out mentors who supported my own developmental needs and goals. I've had three extraordinary mentors, each of whom offered me succinct lessons that are still with me today. Most importantly, I learned that while mentors are helpful *Partners in Power*, they may not always say what you want to hear.

Kathy, my first mentor, was a very successful senior executive in a nationally ranked company. She was a woman of immense fortitude. Amidst her rise to corporate fortune and power, Kathy was fighting a monumental personal battle. She had multiple sclerosis. She shared her stories of conquering real challenges, and with an iron hand and a tender heart, she listened to me recount the professional struggles that were uppermost in my mind. Then she taught me something *really important.*

I remember complaining to Kathy during lunch one day that my job was so *hard* because of some difficulties that I had with some of the people with whom I worked. Kathy abruptly stopped my tirade to tell me about the day she sat in her wheelchair in her bathroom for eight hours while, with trembling malfunctioning hands, she learned to put toothpaste on a toothbrush successfully.

Even though, in her role as my confidant, she was there to empathize with my challenges, with a special finesse and well-timed execution, she altered my perception of what was "hard to do." I gained a new sense of perspective – life is hard when you can't walk, physically care for yourself, or you are living with the impending possibility of death. Kathy taught me about relevance. My challenges were not of great importance in the overall scheme of things. I shifted my attitude to embrace the inherent learning in difficult situations and moved forward from a place of stagnation.

Paul was a short-term mentor who gave me great wisdom in one situation. His profound insight has stayed with me now for 15 years. When I complained to Paul that I faced opposition in my job and that I felt that I was in the "right" against those who had a different belief, he simply said, "You are not paid to be *right*; you are being paid to avoid and solve problems." What I quickly realized was that my need to be right caused more problems than it solved.

Dan has been my mentor and friend for 10 years now. He rides the waves of my professional career and personal life. I met Dan at a corporate event and soon realized that I had previously interviewed with him when I graduated from business school. In our initial exchange, I questioned him as to why he had not hired me for the job several years before. When he quickly retorted, "You did not ask for the job," I knew Dan had something valuable to offer me.

In the course of a turbulent period of my career, Dan worked with me on gaining strength to make good decisions. He taught me the value of moving on and giving up my desire to "fix" situations over which I had no control. We had a playful component to our partnership, even amidst his serious counsel on how to strategically develop and grow. Whenever I left a position, Dan bought dinner. When I successfully secured a new opportunity, I bought dinner! Throughout the years, Dan has celebrated both my increased ability to navigate the corporate community and my consistent growth.

Each of these mentoring encounters centered on values and how to live life authentically. The exchange of knowledge was dynamically reciprocal. What I learned is that successful mentoring partnerships always offer lessons that facilitate and advance the opportunity to live a more balanced and healthy life. *The teacher appears when the student is ready.*

Mentoring is a gift of conversations – conversations that create visions and that allow individuals to embrace the possibility of their dreams. Simply put, mentoring is a series of powerful conversations. Mentoring is most powerful when the conversations transition you away from your status quo by revealing possibilities for the future. In the course of our normal day, we experience routine and, sometimes, restraint. Many of us live with daily pressures from our jobs, relationships and personal life. A day can present challenges, chaos, confusion and, sometimes, competition. When we live with this pressure, our capacity for envisioning possibility is decreased. When we live within the confines of normality, we can become resigned and limited, and we may lose our ability to dream.

> **Mentoring is a gift of conversations that allow individuals to embrace the possibility of their dreams.**

Mentoring conversations can help us regain our foothold, our awareness of possibility. Powerful conversations with people we admire and respect can generate passion, energy and creativity. We have all had spontaneous brainstorming conversations with friends – the kind of casual discussions where we share our perspectives on life's difficulties or personal challenges. Often we come away from these discussions with new energy and ideas for possible problem resolution. New possibilities can arise from these free-flowing exchanges. When creativity and ideas are nurtured or refined by others, our confidence increases, and our dream becomes more profound. With this type of encouragement, our vision advances toward reality. This type of dialogue occurs in mentoring partnerships with trusted advisors.

Any mentor whom you choose will be a personal gift – customized to your needs. Your personal achievement and success do not have to be accomplished alone. You can utilize many diverse resources to grow and gain. When you explore new opportunities, you may have to test new behaviors and adapt creative strategies to produce new and different results. Your mentor can be the mirror against which you reflect and reform your ways. Within the context of trust, confidentiality and safety, you can "try on" new behaviors to see the "fit." You can practice new "strokes," much like the amateur golfer or tennis player does as he revises his swing under the tutelage of a trusted pro. However, be aware that new strategies for growth can temporarily knock you off-balance and momentarily increase your insecurity or dampen your enthusiasm. That is when a mentor can be most encouraging and influential.

As you pursue your path to personal power and take action toward your goals, I invite you to seek out mentors and enjoy the gifts that are inherent in quality partnerships. By definition, mentoring can be a spontaneous or sustained relationship that offers you guidance and nurturing from someone you trust and who cares about you. Your company may offer formal mentoring or coaching as tools for your development. If so, I encourage you to participate when the opportunity arises.

You can also choose to engage in an informal mentoring partnership to reap the same benefits that the formal mentoring model offers. Understand that the foundational elements of a quality partnership, the nature of different types of objectives for mentoring, and the roles of both the mentor and mentee are all important to the success of the partnership. In addition, having an outline that defines the process for recruiting, managing, and evaluating the relationship will further enhance its probability of success.

While you will have the opportunity to learn a great deal about yourself from a good mentor, it is important that you embrace your full identity, your values and your emotional needs before you embark on this excursion. When selecting a person to serve as your mentor, it is imperative that he or she shares your personal values. If not, there may be a loss of respect and trust that could derail the partnership.

In order for mentoring to be effective, it must honor confidentiality. When it is safe to dream and discuss, our ideas become less inhibited and more abundant. Confidential conversations build a safe foundation for dreaming. A solid mentoring foundation is built on trust. When we feel secure we share. Newly developed visions are often unstructured and not well-formed; they are like a rough, uncut diamond in need of polishing and refinement.

To confidently express your visions, you must have the assurance that there is a safety zone surrounding them. Confidential mentoring conversations can infuse your dreams with stability and strength. A trusted mentor can guide you to effectively create the structure in which to develop your dreams into refined action plans. Mentoring is a valuable way to successfully explore your dreams and build possibility and opportunity into your life.

It is not recommended that a person serve as a mentor if he or she has direct or indirect managerial responsibility for you in your current job. Within the context of mentoring, you may be likely to discuss your developmental needs, and it has been shown that it is almost impossible for a mentor who is also a manager to distinguish between what he/she has observed on the job and what has been confided during mentoring conversations. A manager has the responsibility for performance evaluation and, therefore, it is not advisable to ask him or her to serve as an informal mentor.

Eight Steps to Developing a Successful Mentoring Partnership

1. Determine why you need a mentor.
2. Select an ideal mentor.
3. Recruit a mentor.
4. Determine the boundaries of the relationship.
5. Understand roles.
6. Set goals and meeting agendas.
7. Evaluate progress.
8. Bring partnership to a close.

As a mentee, YOU must drive the partnership. You must accept responsibility for setting expectations and ground rules, training the mentor on his/her role, setting the objectives and agenda, as well as managing the two-way communication process that promotes learning and growth. There are eight important steps for developing a successful and rewarding mentoring partnership.

In effective mentoring partnerships, both participants can learn through reciprocal conversations, feedback and sharing. Two-way learning presents an opportunity for both people to learn about giving and receiving.

THE EIGHT STEPS TO DEVELOPING A SUCCESSFUL MENTORING PARTNERSHIP

1. Determine why you need a mentor.

To begin the process of creating a mentoring partnership, the first question you need to ask is: Why do I need a mentor? Assess your readiness and determine your needs. If you have done a thorough inventory of your values and emotional needs, and if you have begun the process of crafting your vision for the future, there should be plenty of material from which to help identify why you want a mentor. There are many reasons why people ask mentors to partner with them in pursuit of personal and professional goals. Some of the more common reasons include:

- Supporting work and life balance goals
- Building and expanding a professional network
- Enhancing leadership development
- Improving interpersonal skills
- Facilitating better communication in relationships
- Navigating corporate culture
- Planning career strategies
- Resolving current work-related challenges
- Learning new problem-resolution skills
- Developing new perspectives and expanding possibilities

2. Select an ideal mentor.

To choose the best mentor for your present situation, make a list of the goals for mentoring and your current needs. Then write down all of the qualities and characteristics that an ideal mentor would possess to help you reach your goals. What kind of personal and professional experience would they have? Think in terms of family background, gender, age, and cultural similarities and differences. Sometimes choosing someone who is different from you but has qualities and characteristics that you admire produces greater growth and will expand your perspective more effectively than someone who is quite similar. Talk to friends, family and business associates to get recommendations by sharing with them some of the qualities and experiences you value in a mentor. When you have developed a list of several potential mentors, evaluate your choices and prioritize your preferences.

3. Recruit a mentor.

Once you have clarified your purpose for mentoring (goals and objectives) and outlined the reason why you think someone would be a good mentor, you have everything you need to recruit the right person. Asking someone to be your mentor – to support your development in a sustained, consistent manner – requires a direct and clear approach. Make sure you set up enough time to ask someone (in person, preferably) to partner with you. Let the individual know why you are seeking his or her help. Articulate your reasons for choosing that person as a mentor. Don't be shy with compliments and expressions of what you admire most about the person. People respond well to sincere compliments about what you admire most about them being a mentor. Lastly, it is important to present a general scope of the partnership (length of commitment, how often you would like to meet, request for honest feedback, and the types of goals you are hoping to achieve) so that the person is on the same page as you when/if they accept your request for support.

4. Determine the boundaries of the relationship.

This is the place where confidentiality, honest communication and trust are presented as the hallmarks of a successful mentoring partnership. Be clear with your desires and expectations and ask for agreement that your mentor will honor your wishes. Next develop the protocol for when, where and how often you will meet with your mentor. These detailed decisions are highly personal to each different partnership. Some mentors and mentees meet during the business day, some at a lunch meeting; others get together more informally after work for a drink, tennis or racquet ball game, sporting event, or even dinner. What you do is not important, but making sure the design of the meetings is comfortable and convenient for both parties is. When you plan your meeting schedule, aim for consistency, and plan a routine that is least likely to be broken due to travel, work or family commitments. Take the time during this first session to discuss your respective styles. Do you want candid, straightforward feedback? Do you want your mentor to challenge you and be aggressive with his/her recommendations for how you can stretch yourself and grow? Are you already overwhelmed at work and just need time to talk through your emotions and internal conflicts? What do you expect from your mentor, and what does your mentor expect from you?

5. Understand roles.

As previously stated, it is important to recognize that the mentee is the one who drives the mentoring partnership. As the mentee, it should be your goals, your agenda, and your responsibility for managing the relationship. You need to have clear expectations of what you want and how you are going to ask for it. Once you have set guidelines, established the schedule, and discussed the boundaries, it is your responsibility to take action if the mentor is not meeting his/her commitments as mutually agreed. Learning to communicate, even in difficult situations, is one of the valuable lessons learned through mentoring.

- A good mentee is organized, proactive, asks for what she needs, comes prepared to meetings, shows respect for her mentor's time, follows up with assignments and recommended tasks, shows appreciation, and stays committed to her growth and development. For the greatest impact, a mentee will stretch beyond her comfort zone and will ask the mentor to challenge her. Taking an honest inventory of one's strengths and developmental areas, she should be willing to listen and learn to improve skills, attitudes and behavior.

- A good mentor also demonstrates excellent listening techniques and uses the art of questioning to probe deeper to allow the mentee to learn more about himself. A mentor does not need to give advice; instead he/she should encourage and practice good problem-solving skills with the mentee. Candid feedback is a must and, when appropriate, the mentor should qualify an observation with "This is just my opinion based on my experience." It will be up to the mentee to respond to, reflect on, or accept a mentor's perspective. A good mentor does not have to have all the answers. Serving as a resource and networking agent are valuable components of the role. Willingness to share one's personal story and professional experiences – including challenges and the key elements of knowledge gleaned from life's experiences – are important attributes of a quality mentor. Commitment, above all, is the key to success. The partnership should be dynamically reciprocal, and the mentor will always have an opportunity for improvement if the mentee is prepared and willing to give candid feedback.

6. Set goals and meeting agendas.

When you recruit your mentor, you should give him/her an overview of your reasons for wanting a mentor. Early in the partnership it is a good idea to formalize your objectives and prioritize (with your mentor) specific goals. You should discuss whether or not to have formal or informal meetings and whether an agenda is something he/she would like to see in advance. As a coach, I always summarize my client's objectives after our first session, and in subsequent sessions I repeatedly refer back to that list to make sure we are on task and moving forward. Ask your mentor for other ideas on how to structure as well as evaluate goals throughout the partnership. He/she may have also had an informal mentor, and you may learn new ideas from his/her experience.

7. Evaluate progress.

When you set your goals for the partnership, you hopefully will build in an evaluation mechanism for how to assess progress. On a consistent basis, it is imperative that you both give candid feedback on how the partnership is going. If either one feels that the meetings are not meaningful or productive, there is likely to be a derailment or cessation of the partnership. It is recommended to plan in advance for a defined endpoint of the relationship (six to twelve months are typical timeframes) and to choose a midpoint at which you will more formally evaluate progress against goals and desired outcomes. If either party feels a need to change the dynamics of the relationship, it is easier to confront at the midpoint when you are formally setting time aside to make improvements for even greater success. The final evaluation may, in fact, be a decision to continue the partnership because it has been successful and/or you are on a positive path to personal power. A final evaluation is a nice summation that gives the mentor feedback on his ability to coach and communicate and offers the mentee final reflections on achievements or continued areas for development.

8. Bring partnership to a close.

This component of the mentoring partnership is highly personal and, depending on the quality of the relationship, can prove to be celebratory or insignificant. At a minimum, demonstrate appreciation and acknowledge the mentor's gifts of time. If you thought the mentor was particularly good at listening, coaching, offering strategic options, serving as a resource, etc., then by all means communicate his or her strengths at the conclusion of your formal time together. These are gifts of praise that a mentor will keep and cherish. Lastly, feel free to discuss informally keeping the partnership alive with a periodic or annual get-together. It is recommended that you clarify if/how your mentor would like to receive your ongoing communication. Some mentors are always willing to receive an additional call for help; others prefer to move on to their next protégé and can only spare time for a periodic luncheon get-together. If you gained insight and sharpened your perception skills throughout the partnership, you will know just how to end or continue this relationship with your partner in power. On a final note, by all means, send your mentor announcements of your career advancements with a special note thanking him/her for his/her part in your success!

BENEFITS OF MENTORING

Whether you choose one mentor or many throughout your life, there are great rewards to be earned from your investment of time in selecting, recruiting and managing a mentor partnership. Consistent with your journey of discovery and the exploration of your potential, a mentor can improve your self-awareness, focus your development, enhance your performance, and strengthen your listening, communication and problem-solving skills. Mentoring partnerships increase your understanding of others as well as support your ability to network and build relationships. The opportunity to build a confidential relationship with a mentor stimulates diversity of thought and can help you be authentic while appreciating differences in others.

A mentor can be the "North Star" in your sky. He/she can be a lighthouse in turbulent waters and temperance in the storm. The secret of mentoring, however, lies with your ability to accept responsibility for piloting the course. It is ultimately your journey, your achievement, and your personal goals toward which you must direct your mentors. It is mandatory that you accept responsibility for steering the course. With mentors in your life, you can more confidently pursue your dreams and successfully live life from a position of power and strength.

Mentors and coaches, like all sources of personal power, are great allies in building the confidence and energy needed to sustain growth. Selecting a *Partner in Power* will be highly personal to each of you.

This chapter has outlined different physical, spiritual and social ways for you to get energized including:

Physical
- Healthy nutrition
- Rest and relaxation
- Physical exercise (energy release or time with nature)

Spiritual
- Meditation or Spiritual Connection
- Intuition (Trusting our Truth)

Social
- Individual Support System (intimate relationships, family and close friends)
- Personal advocates, coaches and mentors

These recommendations are guidelines and suggestions for how you can rejuvenate yourself to connect with life more fully. You may have several other ways that you use to nurture yourself in times of stress. You may have special rituals and daily practices that boost your energy to help maintain a positive attitude. Whatever you prefer, think of your sources of power as part of your vital circle of life. You are at the center of that circle, so surround yourself with the physical, spiritual and social joys that add to your health and well-being.

Discover Your Potential

As you consider your *Partners in Power*, the following questions may be helpful in selecting the ones you will choose to nourish and support your growth.

- What fills you with energy?

- What nourishes you and helps you celebrate life?

- What helps you to feel vibrant and alive?

- What infuses you with a sense of well-being and a positive attitude?

- How do you like to spend time to refresh and revitalize your spirit?

- What gives you the most satisfaction, and what support is missing from your life?

- What can you do to improve your physical health?

- What would you do to improve your spiritual well-being?

- Are you fully engaged with your social connections? How might you enhance your social well-being?

- How often do you seek the support of others who are invested in your growth and development?

- How might you use a coach or mentor to facilitate your commitment to growth and development?

LEADERSHIP POTENTIAL

Imagine a world where all individuals are empowered to develop their full potential. Imagine the strength of an organization that is able to tap into the intellectual capacity, resourcefulness and creativity of its entire workforce. Imagine the employees who are embraced for their innate talents and unique gifts – producing quality results with a profound sense of fulfillment. Imagine these possibilities in your organization and in your life.

Today, people and organizations are being pushed to perform. There are increasing competitive demands for productivity and growth. Leaders are being called upon to guide and inspire their teams to achieve desired results. Effective communication, collaborative teamwork and quality leadership have never been more important.

In response to the critical demand to develop effective leaders, a variety of leadership approaches have been proposed and popularized. Well-known authors and leadership experts such as Peter Senge, Ken Blanchard, Jim Collins and Stephen Covey have offered their own strategies and tools for developing leaders who inspire and empower others to be their best.

All of these contemporary leadership authors identify essential competencies that an individual should possess and practice to be an effective leader. These attributes are vital if one is to become an authentic, strategic, collaborative and visionary leader. Furthermore, many of these prominent leadership approaches are synergistically aligned with the leadership philosophy conceived of by Robert Greenleaf, a retired AT&T executive, in his essay "The Servant as Leader."

His paradoxical term, Servant Leader, has created a quiet revolution and a paradigm shift in management philosophy during the past thirty years. Written in 1970, Greenleaf's thesis highlights characteristics of a leader who successfully serves the needs of others. Upon close examination, the same attributes that Greenleaf espouses are either explicitly or implicitly present in today's most popular leadership training methodologies.

Servant Leadership draws its strength from Greenleaf's premise that "the first and most important choice a leader makes is the choice to serve, without which one's capacity to lead is severely limited." Inherent in this model is the belief that these leaders possess certain quintessential human traits, such as awareness, skilled listening, empathy, and a commitment to the growth of people.

The focus is clearly on serving the needs of others. Leaders who possess these qualities have the ability to recognize the intrinsic value and unique talents of other individuals. Their capacity to affirm other people's self-worth is what initiates growth and unleashes potential.

Before individuals can practice these exemplary leadership principles, they must first operate from a place of authenticity and comprehensive self-awareness. Only then can they transcend to positions of authority and effectively lead by serving the needs of others. The most celebrated of the contemporary models of leadership share this underlying principle, and when leaders practice the ideology rooted in these models, the people and organizations they serve have the potential to be transformed.

For this reason, four of the most popularized leadership philosophies – Authentic, Strategic, Collaborative and Servant – form the foundational components of a new leadership paradigm called the **Cornerstones of Leadership**, a model that was developed as an outgrowth of the principles presented in this book.

As we discovered, in the process of developing potential, individuals need awareness of their Identity, Authenticity, Vision and Actions. Not only are these essential concepts imperative for achieving individual potential, they are also crucial requirements for exceptional leadership.

Furthermore, leaders need the ability to communicate effectively, build collaborative relationships, and strategically move their team forward in today's competitive and challenging business environment. These competencies build upon the basic skills of communication and commitment to action that have been explored in this book.

The four quadrants of the **Cornerstones of Leadership** model are interrelated and interdependent. This paradigm proposes that individuals need to develop all four sets of competencies to be exemplary leaders. *(At the end of this chapter is a self-assessment tool that you can use to evaluate your development as an exemplary leader.)*

CORNERSTONES OF LEADERSHIP

Authentic Leadership *Identity & Authenticity*	Strategic Leadership *Vision & Action*
• Possesses Self-Awareness • Models Ethical Values • Demonstrates Integrity • Displays Professionalism • Exudes Confidence	• Focuses on Vision • Strategically Drives Results • Displays Creativity and Innovation • Plans and Acts Decisively • Solves Problems Resourcefully
Collaborative Leadership *Communication & Collaboration*	Servant Leadership *Mission & Purpose*
• Communicates Effectively • Develops Quality Relationships • Builds Teams and Coalitions • Delegates and Shares Responsibility • Negotiates Conflict	• Serves Mission of the Organization • Creates a Culture of Accountability • Pursues Growth Opportunities • Empowers Others to Be Their Best • Leads with Moral Authority

Authentic Leadership skills include possessing self-awareness, modeling ethical values, demonstrating integrity, displaying professionalism and exuding confidence. All of these competencies align with the basic concepts presented in this book's chapters on Identity and Authenticity. These competencies relate to individuals' awareness of values and emotional needs and their ability to be authentic and possess confidence.

Collaborative Leadership competencies specifically relate to communication and collaboration proficiency. To demonstrate Collaborative Leadership skills, an individual needs to communicate effectively, develop quality relationships, build teams and coalitions, delegate and share responsibility, and have the ability to successfully negotiate conflict. It stands to reason that competency as an authentic leader is a precursor to mastering collaborative leadership skills.

Strategic Leadership skills such as focusing on vision, strategically driving results, displaying creativity and innovation, planning and acting decisively, and solving problems resourcefully correlate with various elements discussed in the Vision and Action chapters in this book. A strategic leader has the ability to conceptualize a vision, progress toward a goal, and successfully maneuver within a structure to take definitive action in order to achieve the desired results.

Servant Leadership is at the core of this model. It also can be viewed as the highest order of competence. The five leadership competencies delineated in this quadrant of the **Cornerstones of Leadership** paradigm correlate to the concepts of mission and purpose. In the Action chapter, we explored mission statements and the concept of a life purpose that guides our development and actions in life.

Robert Greenleaf states that "The servant-leader is servant *first*. It begins with the natural feeling that one wants to serve. Then conscious choice brings one to aspire to lead." Leading by serving is therefore ingrained in the natural mission and purpose of a Servant Leader. Pursuing growth opportunities and empowering others to be their best may be part of an individual's life purpose and, as such, it helps develop an exemplary leader who serves the mission of the organization and ultimately leads with Moral Authority.

There is a cyclical nature built into the **Cornerstones of Leadership** model. As individuals increase their self-awareness to live authentically in alignment with their values, vision and higher purpose, they are more likely to pursue relationships and opportunities that fulfill their emotional needs. Additionally, as individuals become more sentient, with increased awareness of their identity, authenticity, vision and actions, they lay the *cornerstones* or a foundation for growth and development of leadership potential.

As they develop their potential and make choices that successfully fulfill their emotional needs, these individuals enhance their ability for what Maslow calls "Transcendence," which comes only after individual needs are fully satisfied. Transcendence involves rising above satisfying one's own needs and evolving to a place where "giving back" or satisfying the needs of others is more desirable.

I call this phenomenon the **Potential of Leadership**, meaning that as you achieve your potential you are well-positioned to be an exemplary leader helping to unleash the potential of others. There is also a paradoxical **Promise of Leadership** inherent in this model: as you serve others you will, in effect, serve yourself.

Therefore, given the potential inherent in this exemplary leadership paradigm, the opportunity exists for each of you, as you reach your *potential*, to become the kind of leader who nourishes and develops the people you serve. And, as described in the *promise* of leading by serving, you will discover that in the process of nurturing the needs of others, you will nourish yourself. As the reciprocal cycle suggests, when you give to (serve) others, you have the potential to give to (serve) yourself.

To illustrate how leadership can have reciprocal rewards, consider the following story of a young woman who volunteered as a leader in a nonprofit agency:

Wendy was midway through her career when she decided that she needed to "give back" and share some of what she learned with women who were either at the beginning of their career or amidst a life or career transition. While Wendy always worked hard in all her personal and professional endeavors, she had the tendency to underestimate her own worth and competency. At times, even after many years of success, she struggled to remain confident and secure in her performance and career. Even so, she decided it was time to rise above her own needs and consider helping others.

Wendy selected a small women's agency called *The Coaching Clinic* for her volunteer commitment. She met with the clinic's management staff, gave them her resumé, and said she would consult in whatever capacity they felt best matched her experience with the organization's needs. The staff suggested that Wendy would be a great leader and trainer for one of their business courses. After reviewing the materials for the course, Wendy agreed that she not only had experience in the business services outlined in the class, but she had a passion for the subject matter as well.

Wendy began teaching the class with the same feeling of trepidation with which she approached every new venture. She questioned her ability and wondered if she would be an effective trainer and role model for the students. An hour into the first evening, her fear subsided; Wendy relaxed and began to enjoy herself with a new sense of assurance. Ultimately, she genuinely cared about her students, compassionately listened to their questions, and enthusiastically supported their development. In return, the students were attentive, receptive to her suggestions, and most of all, they were appreciative of her time and experience. The final evaluations for her course validated that Wendy was a very effective instructor who exhibited many of the qualities of admirable leadership.

Upon reflection, Wendy realized that in her role as a volunteer leader, she felt more valued and recognized as a person than in any other circumstance in her life. She felt connected to her students, loved volunteer training, and always looked forward to her time at *The Coaching Clinic*. Even after a full day at her professional job, Wendy always left the clinic feeling renewed and refreshed!

Wendy's story is similar to many people who volunteer and give of themselves to community agencies, church groups, and other nonprofit organizations. Wendy's feelings of being valued, connected, and effective validated the reciprocity embedded in this leadership concept: When people fulfill the needs of others, they replenish and fulfill their own needs as well.

Perhaps you can identify with Wendy because you have experienced a similar sense of gratification from volunteering or donating your time to support the development of others. Or possibly, you have had a manager who displayed comparable qualities when they were working with you. The following contrasting illustrative examples of two types of leaders may trigger other reflections of people with whom you have worked.

CASE STUDY 1: *Barry, the Bad Boss*
Barry was a veteran sales professional with more than 20 years of experience as an individual contributor and manager for a Fortune 500 company. He was an aggressive, hard-driving, results-oriented person who demanded a great deal from each of his employees. Barry had a reputation for impatience and very direct, forceful communication. As a result of a company reorganization, Barry became the new manager for a regional sales team consisting of seven seasoned sales executives.

Immediately after Barry became her boss, Traci, a top-notch salesperson, suddenly left the company. Oliver, in Ohio, transferred to another division after two weeks of Barry's incessant demands and condescending remarks. John and Jay both worked in another Midwest office and compared notes regularly about how rude, insensitive and disrespectful Barry was to them.

Jade was the oldest and most experienced employee reporting to Barry. She also was the recipient of his most abusive and incessant requests. Within a month of becoming her boss and after meeting her in person only twice, Barry delivered a performance improvement plan (by e-mail) to Jade that threatened termination if his requirements were not met.

Even though Jade had received a very positive performance review from her previous boss, Barry never recognized any of her efforts, nor did he take the time to discuss his expectations with her. Furthermore, he did not offer any support to help her meet his demands within the specified time frame. Jade was frustrated and fearful.

Jade thought Barry's actions were unwarranted and unfair so she contacted an attorney to review her situation. After careful consideration of all the facts, the lawyer told Jade that he agreed Barry was abusive and that she was, indeed, the victim of unfair treatment. Unfortunately, he concluded that Jade did not have a legal case against Barry because the discrimination did not appear to relate to her age, gender, race or religion. Therefore, it was permissible by law. Barry's behavior was not illegal; it was just incompetent and uncaring. Barry was the kind of leader who did not demonstrate any compassion or concern for the human beings whom he managed.

Ultimately, after many tears and immense feelings of failure, Jade left the company before Barry could fire her. She silently admonished herself for not meeting Barry's demands even though she knew in her heart that they were unrealistic and could not have been achieved by anyone. Within a short time, she regained enough confidence to secure another position for which she was better suited.

Many months later, while enjoying her new job, she circled back to talk with a friend from the old company and discovered that she was not the only person who was successfully "out from under Barry's thumb." All seven of Barry's direct reports had left the company within the first year of his management rule. Jade secretly smiled when she learned that at least two of them expressed their disgust for Barry's incompetence during the exit interviews with human resources.

While Barry, the Bad Boss, is an extreme example, contrast his lack of leadership competencies with those described in the next case study.

CASE STUDY 2: *Eleanor, the Empowering Entrepreneur*
Eleanor was the entrepreneurial CEO of a small start-up business venture focusing on executive education and development services. She hired Jackie to join the company as the Director of Business Development the fifth year the company was in business. Eleanor's company was successful and had an excellent reputation for its products and services in the local business community. Jackie's role was to help Eleanor expand the company nationwide.

Jackie was new to the industry, and while she had an MBA in marketing, most of her business development experience came from positions she held in nonprofit organizations. Yet, she had a passion for professional development and loved the types of programs that Eleanor's company offered to support executive education.

From the very first day when she joined Eleanor's company, Jackie was recognized for the energy and enthusiasm she brought to her position. Eleanor knew that Jackie lacked "hands-on" experience in marketing to Fortune 500 companies, but she still complimented Jackie's innate skills and dedicated herself to helping Jackie learn the business to gain the confidence she needed to be successful.

Eleanor was a warm and compassionate communicator. She spent hours getting to know Jackie and sharing stories – both personal and professional – to strengthen their relationship and to increase the new woman's knowledge of the company, its programs, and its history of success. Eleanor had an open-door policy and patiently answered the plethora of questions that Jackie presented. She also acknowledged and praised Jackie for the depth of her inquiry and the organized approach she implemented getting up to speed.

In the first few months of Jackie's employ, she felt highly appreciated and valued. Surprisingly, she was even more motivated to perform. She was a self-motivated high-achiever and yet, with Eleanor's expressed confidence in her abilities, Jackie wanted to succeed even more. Early in her tenure with the company, Jackie was talking about her personal financial goals with Eleanor, and she openly acknowledged what she hoped to make, in terms of total compensation, for her sales efforts with the company. Much to Jackie's surprise, Eleanor raised the bar even higher by saying, "You will make more money than you expect! You are going to be so successful here. I can already tell by your energy and enthusiasm."

Eleanor's declaration proved to be right, and Jackie spent five very lucrative years with the company. Not only did she earn great financial rewards while she worked for Eleanor, but Jackie profitably developed her skills and confidence as well. Under Eleanor's leadership, Jackie learned to trust her instincts, stretch herself toward higher goals, and take risks in performing beyond her comfort zone. The results were self-evident when Jackie, and the company, achieved great success.

All of the employees who reported to Eleanor in those early years were embraced for their innate talents and skills, just like Jackie. All were encouraged to perform because they were valued members of the team that complemented Eleanor's vision of creating a nationally recognized company. Eleanor knew that the people she employed were critical to her success – without them, she would not reach her goals. She dedicated herself to helping them grow, nurturing their individual potential, and then watching them flourish and succeed.

Jackie and her teammates were recognized for everything that they did, regardless of whether or not they achieved a final goal. This motivated them to do more. In addition to showing appreciation for their efforts, Eleanor remained open to their ideas, respected their contributions, and celebrated their contributions to her company. Her number one message was "I value you as a person," and from that empowering communication, each employee consistently performed at the highest level of capability.

This evaluation of exemplary leadership brings us full circle to the beginning of this book. To release talent and potential, we need to affirm the whole person. We need awareness of the individual's full identity, we need to embrace his or her authenticity, and we need to appreciate and support the individual's vision with our actions.

As we have seen throughout this book, fulfillment of emotional needs is directly related to performance and personal satisfaction. Whether you are an individual striving to reach your professional vision or a leader hoping to tap into the innate talents of your employees, achieving the competencies associated with the **Cornerstones of Leadership** will deliver the promise of the potential you desire.

Moreover, if you are an individual seeking to grow, develop and reach your full potential, it is essential that you receive the empowering encouragement of this type of leader to support your quest. By example, "Barry, the Bad Boss" batters self-esteem, diminishes motivation, and reduces productivity and results. In contrast, "Eleanor, the Empowering Entrepreneur" knows what is really most important in leading employees to develop their capabilities.

The exemplary leader understands it's about *helping* people be more effective, collaborative, successful and confident. It is about affirming the individual worth of every person and setting up systems and structures to ensure that all employees are valued and recognized for their authentic being.

To accomplish this goal, the best leaders and organizations know that they must shift from the old management paradigm of "command and control" to "position for potential" to create a culture that cultivates and encourages employees. Unleashing potential is just as it sounds – taking the "harnesses" off to set people free to be the best that they can be. These leaders shift away from power to *position for possibility* by fostering, promoting and developing potential.

As you consider the **Cornerstones of Leadership** model and think about how you can apply this to your life, know that you are well-positioned to recognize and become the kind of leader who nurtures the development and potential of others. As you reflect on what you have read and the exercises you have completed, know that these sound principles and valuable tools can be used to support and empower others.

Most of what you have learned about becoming aware of your own values and emotional needs can be applied to helping others learn about themselves. You can use the mentoring, coaching and communication techniques presented in this book to engage in empowering conversations to promote the growth of people you support.

The "I AM / I NEED / I WANT / I WILL" model is a great way to acknowledge unique talents and gifts and to explore individual needs. Further, the **Circle of Communication** tool can initiate effective discussions to increase the potential for creating shared visions and formulating a mutual commitment to action.

As you reflect on the leaders who have helped you the most and the people who have devoted themselves to your growth, you may naturally emulate their compassionate leadership style because you now implicitly understand how essential it is to embrace people for who they are and to acknowledge their authenticity and emotional needs. Because you are a unique being, a multifaceted diamond with your own special strengths and gifts, you may want to personalize these guiding leadership principles to work for you.

You have been given the opportunity of a lifetime – to cultivate your innate gifts and strengths, to explore your dreams and aspirations, and to achieve a sense of fulfillment from all that you accomplish. As you have learned, to discover your full potential, you must *first* look deep within. With genuine appreciation for the magnificent being that you are, you gain the ability to live authentically and the capacity to share what you have learned with others.

Just as your life will continue to be a journey, your experience as a leader will unfold and blossom over time. You may also discover that your success will result from four fundamental characteristics: understanding, wisdom, strength and faith. Hopefully, as you come to understand and embrace yourself and nourish your own needs, you will gain the wisdom and strength to nurture others. Moreover, have faith that your transcendence will bring you the greatest contentment and peace you have ever known.

In conclusion, what is most important is that we all must dedicate ourselves to this cycle of developing the promise of potential in ourselves and in others. In so doing, there will be a continuous process of awareness and fulfillment. As we transcend to become sentient beings who lead by serving others, we will nourish ourselves and achieve the ultimate possibility… *a world where all individuals are empowered to develop the full promise of their potential.*

Discover Your Potential

Cornerstones of Leadership Self-Assessment

For each of these qualities, evaluate your competence using the following scale:

(+) Strength   (–) Developmental   (O) Demonstrates Occasionally

AUTHENTIC LEADERSHIP: *Identity & Authenticity*

_____ Possesses Self-Awareness

_____ Models Ethical Values

_____ Demonstrates Integrity

_____ Displays Professionalism

_____ Exudes Confidence

STRATEGIC LEADERSHIP: *Vision & Action*

_____ Focuses on Vision

_____ Strategically Drives Results

_____ Displays Creativity and Innovation

_____ Plans and Acts Decisively

_____ Solves Problems Resourcefully

COLLABORATIVE LEADERSHIP: *Communication & Collaboration*

_____ Communicates Effectively

_____ Develops Quality Relationships

_____ Builds Teams and Coalitions

_____ Delegates and Shares Responsibility

_____ Negotiates Conflict

SERVANT LEADERSHIP: *Mission & Purpose*

_____ Serves Mission of the Organization

_____ Creates a Culture of Accountability

_____ Pursues Growth Opportunities

_____ Empowers Others to Be Their Best

_____ Leads with Moral Authority

NOTES:

Strengths:

_____

_____

_____

_____

Development Opportunities:

_____

_____

_____

_____

Action Goals:

_____

_____

_____

_____

LINKS TO POTENTIAL

The authors and leadership references cited in this chapter are listed below.

- Ken Blanchard: www.KenBlanchard.com

- *Good to Great: Why Some Companies Make the Leap... and Others Don't* by Jim Collins

- *The 7 Habits of Highly Effective People* by Stephen Covey www.FranklinCovey.com

- *The 8th Habit: From Effectiveness to Greatness* by Stephen Covey www.FranklinCovey.com

- *Principle-Centered Leadership* by Stephen Covey www.FranklinCovey.com

- *The Fifth Discipline: The Art & Practice of the Learning Organization* by Peter M. Senge

Servant Leadership Resources and References

- The Greenleaf Center for Servant Leadership: www.Greenleaf.org

- *The Servant as Leader,* an essay by Robert K. Greenleaf

- *Servant Leadership: A Journey into the Nature of Legitimate Power and Greatness* by Robert Greenleaf, Larry C. Spears, and Stephen R. Covey

- *Robert K. Greenleaf: A Life of Servant Leadership* by Don M. Frick, Peter M. Senge, and Larry C. Spears

ABOUT THE AUTHOR

Jodi Davis learned firsthand the essential need to look deep within for the strength and confidence to be authentic and to pursue dreams in the face of adversity. When her young daughter died following open-heart surgery, Jodi was catapulted into a new phase of adulthood and a personal quest to discover her own potential.

Jodi's new developmental journey began at age 34 with an appointment to the Board of Directors of the Children's Hospital, an acceptance to Graduate Business School, and a divorce ending her 15-year marriage. As a single parent of three small children, she accepted these early challenges with a thirst for knowledge and an eagerness to discover her strengths and gifts that would lead to a life of fulfillment.

Her twenty-year professional career has included corporate positions as a sales and marketing executive and management professional. She served as the Executive Director of a children's fund for the University of Minnesota, held sales positions with several Fortune 1000 companies, and is the former Senior Vice President of Menttium Corporation, the nation's leading authority on corporate mentoring programs.

Her diverse career positions brought with them many rewards and hardships that ultimately contributed to her enhanced understanding of human development. During the good times, Jodi had extraordinary managers and mentors, growth opportunities, and financial recognition. The difficult situations included incompetent and unfair bosses, the sudden loss of a cherished job, and a company-wide layoff.

As a result of these varied experiences, Jodi ultimately pursued training and certification as a coach and human potential trainer. In 2001, she founded JD Coaching and Consulting, an organization development firm that helps individuals, teams and organizations improve leadership performance and effectiveness.

Jodi Davis holds an MBA from St. Thomas University in Minneapolis/St. Paul, Minnesota, and a B.S. in Education from the University of Minnesota. She received her professional training from the Coaches Training Institute (CTI), and she is certified as a human potential trainer by the internationally recognized Empowerment Institute in New York. She is currently an adjunct professor for the Minneapolis College of Art & Design and a volunteer consultant for WomenVenture in St. Paul, Minnesota.

Jodi's first book, *The Heart's Gift* (©2003), is an inspiring story of love, hope and renewal – a courageous account of facing and enduring one of life's most tragic events – her infant daughter's serious illness and death. An engaging speaker, Jodi enjoys sharing her story to empower others to embrace their life vision and full potential. She currently lives in Minneapolis and enjoys her three grown children, twin grandchildren and Shih Tzu dogs, Belle-e-button and Martini.